Kabbalah
365

Kabbalah
365

Daily Fruit from
the Tree of Life

BY GERSHON WINKLER

Foreword by
Andrew Weil, M.D.

Andrews McMeel
Publishing

Kansas City

04 05 06 07 08 FFG 10 9 8 7 6 5 4 3 2 1

Library of Congress Cataloging-in-Publication Data

Kabbalah 365 : daily fruit from the tree of life / Gershon Winkler ; foreword by Andrew Weil.
    p. cm.
  Includes index.
  ISBN 0-7407-4720-7
    1. Cabala—Translations into English. 2. Rabbis—Anecdotes—Translations into English. 3. Rabbinical literature—Translations into English. I. Winkler, Gershon, 1949-

  BM525.A2K32 2004
  296.1'6—dc22

2004049085

To Robert A. Levin, whose wisdom
I will always cherish, and
whose vision and generosity
have contributed immensely to
the quality of my life and
that of myriad others

Foreword

By Andrew Weil, M.D.

In my work as a health professional I have found that healing is not so much about fixing as it is about restoring balance and perspective, and getting past old patterns. *Kabbalah 365* is a unique book that I believe can help get us unstuck. Gershon Winkler has gleaned his information from many sources, mostly from ancient and early medieval Hebraic and Aramaic texts, to compile a unique collection of aphorisms and stories. Each daily reading is meant to remind us of the magic of being alive and the profound gifts that each moment can bring. As he does in his workshops and seminars, Rabbi Winkler renders user-friendly the more cryptic teachings of lesser-known Kabbalistic source texts and oral traditions in order to inspire and inform our lives.

Readers of all backgrounds, religious or not, will discover in this book a body of wisdom that shows that nothing is etched in stone and everything is far more than it appears. Moreover, these teachings and parables free up our imagination, enabling us to discover, each in his or her own individual way our *own* Kabbalistic experience of the magic of this life. *Kabbalah* literally means "Receiving." It exists to encourage us to remain always open to receive anew the wisdom that waits to be discovered in ourselves, in each other, and in the beings with whom we share this planet.

I have long been drawn to the Kabbalah but have rarely found the time and stamina to wade through the few available English renditions of its dense and often cryptic texts. But here, at last, is a book that recasts these very same teachings—including a great many more that I never knew about—into a readable vernacular that remains true to the spirit and intention of the original sources. Did you know, for example, that when birds fly, their wings slice through the ether, allowing divine energies to enter our world? Did you know that if you see an eagle it is a sign of compassion? Did you know that the winds of the four directions gift us with healing, vision, mystery, and balance? Or that the very first thing the Creator made was a rock, and from that rock all of the universe emerged? Did you know that deep within the very obstacles that stand in the way of your journey toward enlightenment is precisely where enlightenment waits to be discovered? These and so many more useful teachings await you within these pages.

PREFACE

The teachings in this book were translated by the author into user-friendly renditions from sources that include but are not limited to the following Aramaic and Hebraic sources: Babylonian Talmud, *Batei Midrashot, Etz Ha'Chayyim,* Jerusalem Talmud, *Kit'vei Ha'Ari, Likuttei Ha'MaHaRaN, M'irat Ey'nayim, Midrash Ha'Heychalot, Midrash HaNe'elam, Midrash Pesik'ta D'Rav Kahana, Midrash Pesik'ta Rabatti, Midrash P'liyah, Midrash Rabbah, Midrash Tanchuma, Midrash Tehilim, Nefesh Ha'Chayyim, Rei'Sheet Choch'mah, Sefer Ha'Bahir, Sefer Ha'Razim, Sefer HaRoke'ach, Sefer Hash'lah Ha'kadosh, Sefer Ha'Zohar, Sefer Ru'ach Ha'Kodesh, Sefer So'day Ra'zeya, Sefer Yetzirah, Shoshan Y'sod Olam, Sif'rei Ha'Maharal, Tanakh,* and various oral traditions.

Introduction

Kabbalah 365 is a unique collection of rare Jewish mystery wisdom gathered mostly from original Hebraic and Aramaic sources. Some are accessible in various English translations; however, most remain untranslated and often in manuscript form, hidden away in academic library archives. These selected readings for every day of the yearly cycle are intended as contemplative, inspirational, and at times entertaining. They are also replete with kernels of wisdom that are pragmatic and timeless, cryptic and evident. Many of these nuggets are presented here for the first time in the English language, and all are phrased in the contemporary vernacular. Even more of them are based largely on lesser-promulgated Kabbalistic texts that both teachers and students of the Kabbalah will find fresh and unparalleled in their studies to date.

The Kabbalah has for millennia been an integral body of wisdom largely responsible for inspiring and fostering the dynamic quality of Judaism's oral and written traditions. Through the most trying times in Jewish history, it was the vision of the mystic that stirred aliveness in the soul of the people, and that time and again prevented theological atrophy in a tradition that was repeatedly denigrated by dominant cultures and religions. The Kabbalah moved the devotees of Judaism to explore the Scriptures of their faith beyond their textual contents to discover the soul behind the words, and then the soul behind the soul, ad infinitum. To this day, the Kabbalah challenges linear thinking, and discourages literal meaning and experience as the sole determinants of truth. More than any other body of wisdom, the Kabbalah keeps an ancient tradition from weakening with age, offering instead ever-renewed strength.

It is no wonder, then, that our current era—a product largely of rationalistic, scientific, and "enlightened" paradigms that had all but dismissed mysticism and shamanism—has witnessed a resurgence of interest in the Kabbalah emerging not solely from the Jewish community but also from people of other spiritual and cultural backgrounds. The current return of the human spirit's intrigue with mysticism, whether the Kabbalah or other forms of mystery wisdom, is neither incidental nor coincidental but is rather reflective of the nature of the human spirit. The Kabbalah was born out of the more primitive desire of the human spirit to bask in more than the end-product of life's knowledge and meaning, yearning as well for the gift of the process, the journey, and the ever-unfolding phases of being in this life rather than achieving. True achievement, the Kabbalists realized, is not to be found in the finale of the accomplishment as much as it is to be found in the moment-to-moment mystery that ultimately brings you there.

This book is therefore unique in that it will guide you not toward any particular climax, or "point," or objective, but toward the gift of the moment, of each day—of the single, yet undefined phase of your individual unfolding and of your personal understanding and appreciation of life. Every day of the solar year, you can be awakened by a tidbit of wisdom from the Kabbalah, awakened to the gift of self, the gift of other, the gift of knowing, and even the gift of not knowing. Every page of this book will remind you that there is more to life than life itself, and that there is richness to just being, a richness that knows no boundaries, that has not been fathomed or explored to its fullest, not even by the Kabbalah. Rather, each person contemplating or meditating upon the teachings and stories in this book will be challenged to delve deeper, to expand farther, and to open their heart to receive from what waits to give. After all, *Kabbalah* literally translates as: "Receiving."

DAY 1

When it arose in the Mind of the Infinite to create, the Infinite manifested as Endless Light and encompassed All. In the time beyond time, before there was time, in a moment between moments before there was moment, Infinite Being constricted Its own Essence to allow for the emergence of space. Then, within that clearing, void of Itself, Infinite Being manifested a single ray of Its Endless Light, Its Infinite Presence. And from this single ray, the universe came into being.

—Sixteenth-century Rabbi Chayyim Vital
in *Etz Ha'Chayyim*, Ch. 1

DAY 2

Were God to fill the universe, the universe could not exist. And were God to not fill the universe, the universe could not exist. It is then through perfectly balanced self-limitation that the Infinite One enables the possibility of existence.

DAY 3

All the stars and the planets are beings with soul, replete with knowledge and thought. They are living entities and are conscious of their Creator. Each one, according to their position and greatness, utters praise and gratitude to the Creator in the same manner as the angels. And just as they are aware of God, they are also self-aware. The consciousness of the stars and the planets is lower than that of angels and higher than that of humans.

—Twelfth-century Rabbi Moshe ibn Maimon
in *Mishnah Torah, Hil'chot Y'sodei HaTorah* 3:9

DAY 4

In the beginning, the Source of all Powers—*Elo'heem*—
created something from nothing. Who is the Source of all
Powers? She is the Great Mother—*e'ma d'ila'a*—and she
created three artisans: Water, Sky, and Earth. And she said to
each, "Create something of your essence" and each one did
just that. The water made the fish and all the great whales;
the sky made the stars, the sun, the moon, and all the planets;
the earth made the plants, the trees, and all the animals
and birds.

—*Sefer Ha'Zohar*, Vol. 4, folio 219b

DAY 5

When all had been created, the Great Mother said to all of Creation: "I have one more creature I wish to bring forth. But this one none of you can create alone. It will take all of us together." And so the Great Mother joined with the forces of Water, Sky, and Earth and created Human, and blew into its nostrils the breath of the Four Winds from all four directions, and asked each wind to gift the human with a special attribute.

—*Midrash HaNe'elam,* folio 16b; *Sefer Ha'Zohar,* Vol. 1, folio 61b, and Vol. 2, folios 23b–24a

DAY 6

In the beginning there was Breath of God. From Breath of God came Wind. From Wind came Water. From Water came Fire. From Fire came Sky. From Sky came Earth. From Earth came North Wind. From North Wind came South Wind. From South Wind came East Wind. From East Wind came West Wind.

—*Sefer Yetzirah,* Section One, final *Mishnah*

DAY 7

The Four Winds correspond to the Four Rivers that emerged from the single, unnamed river that flowed through the Garden of Eden: River of Simple Unity, River of Fruition, River of the Mouth of Transformation, and River of the Belly Flow (Genesis 2:10–14). In each of our life journeys, we are to follow these rivers, blending our life walk with simplicity, realization, change, and passion. Following these rivers will lead us to the unnamed wellspring of all Being.

DAY 8

As living entities, the Four Winds possess their own temperament. The east wind is always good and even quiets the other winds when they get out of hand. The west wind is not that good. The south wind is sometimes one, sometimes the other, and the north wind keeps them all in check. Still, the power of the north wind is effective only during the act of tempering the other winds. By itself it could be destructive "rendering even gold as worthless." The south wind is more moody than the others, more often manic. The south is the place of River of Diversity. It is tempered, as are all the other winds, by the north wind, the place of River of Simple Unity, or stillness. And when so tempered, the south wind brings blessing to the earth's yield.

—Babylonian Talmud, *Gittin* 31b, *Yoma* 21b, *Baba Bat'ra* 25a

DAY 9

Once Rabbi Huna and Rabbi Chis'da were sitting together when Geniva happened to pass by. One said to the other: "Let us stand up for him—he is a man of great learning." The other replied: "Shall we stand up for a man who is always arguing?" In the meantime Geniva approached them and asked: "What have you been discussing?" They replied: "The Winds." He said: "Rabbi Chanan bar Rava once quoted Abba Arey'kha as teaching that every day four winds blow, and the north wind blows along with each of them. Were it not so, the world could not continue to exist for a single moment. The south wind is the most violent, and if the hawk spirit did not hold it back, it would destroy the entire world, all of it."

—Babylonian Talmud, *Gittin* 31b and *Baba Bat'ra* 25

DAY 10

Rabbah Bar Bar Chanah (fourth century) was once journeying across the desert when he came upon a Bedouin who said to him: "Come with me, and I shall show you the window to Heaven." When they came to the spot, the rabbi noticed that there were several windows between Earth and Heaven, so he placed his travel provisions in one of the windows and proceeded to pray. When he finished praying he was shocked to discover that his provisions were gone. He asked the Bedouin: "What, are there thieves in Heaven, too?" To which the Bedouin replied: "Heaven is a revolving wheel—wait until tomorrow, and you will see your supplies returning."

—Babylonian Talmud, *Baba Bat'ra* 73b–74a

DAY 11

When you put on your sandals, first lower your foot into the sandal and imagine the connecting of Sky to Earth. Then lift the straps upward to tie them and imagine the meeting and binding of Earth with Sky.

—Sixteenth-century Rabbi Moshe Cordovero in *Ziv'chey Sh'lamim*

DAY 12

Merkavah is the mystery that carries all existence. It is the mystery that carries you right now, that holds you, that steers you, and guides you. *Merkavah* is the embrace of the Four Winds, the four breaths that emanate from the one single primordial breath of God that brings all into existence. In this embrace we are carried as we journey through this lifetime. The literal translation of *mer'kavah* means "to ride," as opposed to walking or running; it means to ride, as in being carried by something else. It means to have faith that you will get there, wherever, whenever.

DAY 13

If you are in a hurry to get to an appointment, and you are riding on a train that is moving too slow, do you think you will arrive at your destination any faster by getting up and running through the train? Likewise, when the time is right for you, you'll be arriving at your destination—no sooner, no later. In the meantime, make sure you are on board.

—Rabbi Eliezer Benseon Bruk; oral tradition

DAY 14

Three sounds are inaudible to the human ear and never leave the earth: the sound of the snake shedding its skin, the sound of a soul leaving the body at death, and the sound of birthing. Where do these sounds go? They travel to the canyons where they encrypt themselves in the earth. The sound of your voice in the canyon awakens them from dormancy and evokes their powers. However, to awaken the sound of the snake shedding its skin, you must tap wood to stone. You hear these sounds as "echoes" but know that they are three sounds coming right back to you in the garb of your own voice or drumming, to empower you with shedding your old patterns, to aid you in surrendering to the uncertainty of your next step, and to guide you in birthing yourself anew.

—Second-century Rabbi Shim'on bar Yo'chai
in *Sefer Ha'Zohar,* Vol. 3, folio 168b

DAY 15

If you are rubbing two sticks together and are having difficulty lighting a fire, move to another place and try again. Likewise, if you are having difficulty in the place where you are, shift to another place.

—*Sefer Ha'Zohar,* Vol. 4, folio 166b

DAY 16

The buzzard wields the magic of restoring life anew, for she carries the breath of life that she has received from a dying creature. Thus, when Abraham our father split in half the heifer, the ram, and the she-goat during his covenantal ceremony, he was visited by a buzzard from whom he received the power to restore these animals to life.

—Nineteenth-century RABBI ME'IR LEIBUSH [*Mal'bum*]
on Genesis 15:11

DAY 17

It is impossible for the earth to exist without the Four Winds.
Rabbi Abayya (fourth century) taught: "It is impossible for
the universe to exist without so much as the fragrance of
the rose."

—*Sefer Ha'Zohar,* Vol. 2, folio 5b and Vol. 2, folio 20a

DAY 18

Corresponding to the four directions, the Wind of *yhwh* is in the North, the Wind of wisdom and understanding is in the West, the Wind of counsel and balance is in the East, and the Wind of knowing and awe of *yhwh* is in the South (Isaiah 11:2). In their manifestation as spirit beings, they are: *Refa'el* to the West, *Meecha'el* to the South, *Gav'ree'el* to the East, and *Uree'el* to the North. Each of these spirit beings describe a particular manifestation of the Creator in the physical universe: *Refa'el* is the healing manifestation, *Meecha'el* is the reflective manifestation, *Gav'ree'el* is the balancing manifestation, and *Uree'el* is the illuminating manifestation. The powers of the four spirit guardians of the Four Winds are therefore healing, reflection, balance, and vision.

—*Midrash Bamid'bar Rabbah* 2:10

DAY 19

Healing is in the West because the west is the place of death, merging, fear, and relationships—items on the list of major things to overcome in order to heal. Reflection is in the South because the south is the place of cleansing, which requires the clarity and discerning power of reflection. Balance is in the East because the east is the place of new beginnings, which happen in a good way when you balance yourself before springing. Vision is in the North because the north is the place of mystery, of the unknown, the place where the Creator steps back, so to speak, in order to create room for your choice, your daring next move in life, which requires clarity of vision and dream.

DAY 20

Upward is *ma'aleh,* or, literally: the Climbing Place, and Downward is *mahtah,* or, literally: the Tribal Place. The life-beings of Upward are of the *tsow'mey'ach,* the "Sprouting Beings" as in trees, grasses, and flowers, whose direction of evolution is skybound. The life beings of Downward are of the *doe'mem,* the "Still Beings" as in stones, mountains, and minerals, whose direction of evolution is earthbound. Flourishing in the spheres between Sky and Earth are the *chayyah,* or "Wild Life," and the *m'dahber,* the "Speaking Beings," or humans.

DAY 21

The ancient Jewish morning prayer *Elo'hi* reminds us that each morning we awaken with a freshly laundered spirit, and that we don't have to start the new day shuffling about with yesterday's toilet paper still stuck to our shoes:

My Source of Power,
the breath that you have given
   into me

She is pure.

You created her,
You formed her,
You blew her into me
And you watch over her within
   my being

and you will one day take her
   from me
and restore her within me
in the time to come;
every moment
that the breath is within me,
I acknowledge my gratitude
   before You,
my Source of power
and the Power of my ancestors,
Master of all Creations,
Keeper of all Souls.

Source of Blessing are You, *yah*,
who restores breath
to the lifeless.

—Babylonian Talmud, *B'rachot* 60b

21

DAY 22

In the moment of lovemaking between a woman and a man, an image in the likeness of a human forms in the mind of the Sacred Wellspring. This image (*diyok'na* in Aramaic) is sculpted around the soul that is designated to become the life-result of this lovemaking. It becomes the vehicle for the soul's journey into the earthly realm and for its journey out of the earthly realm. Very few are capable of seeing this image around the person, which grows with the person as the person evolves and stays with them until the day they die—at which time their soul becomes once again garbed by this image for its journey back to the spirit world. This image is alluded to in the Book of Genesis, as it is written: "And the Source of Powers created the earth being in its image," meaning not in the image of the Source of Powers but in this image of which we now speak. And as it is also written in the Book of Psalms (39:7): "Only by way of the Image shall a person journey." And indeed it is through the vehicle of this image that we journey in our dream and in our double.

—*Sefer Ha'Zohar*, Vol. 3, folio 104b

DAY 23

The Four Winds are interconnected by their earthly attributes, Breath, Water, Fire, and Earth. Breath is in the east, Fire is in the south, Water is in the north, and Earth is in the west. Fire of south and water of north are joined by the attributes of east and west. The dryness of fire in the south is linked to the dryness of earth in the west, and the coldness of earth in the west is linked to the coldness of water in the north. The moisture of water in the north is linked to the moisture of breath in the east, and the warmth of breath in the east is linked to the warmth of fire in the south.

—*Sefer Ha'Zohar,* Vol. 2, folio 24a
[the *Zohar* version has fire in the north and water in the south, but mirroring one another so that the quality of fire in the north is reflected in the south, and the quality of water in the south is reflected in the north]

DAY 24

When you become aware that the wind is blowing at you from the north, open yourself to the gift of imagination, and the gift of fantasy. Pray for the removal of all that impedes you from exploring possibility beyond the givens and definitions that might keep you stuck. Pray for the gift of mystery, the gift of the North Wind.

DAY 25

If the wind is blowing from the east, open yourself to fresh
inspiration trickling toward you, daring you to surrender
to it. Pray for possibility to emanate from the Place of New
Beginning, which is the east; freshen your ideas, and through
new lenses experience the next moment so that your journey
forward is not directed by your rearview mirror.

DAY 26

If the wind is coming from the south, receive the gift of
communication, and the capacity to articulate to yourself and
to others your wildest hopes and dreams. Pray for clarity in
the wind of the south, that what you feel so driven toward
achieving in the world be free of distortion and illusion. Pray
for honesty in your self and in your relationship with others;
come clean and rise—the gift of the south.

DAY 27

If the wind is blowing at you from the west, open your
heart to receive and manifest the gift of realization. Pray for
actualization of what it is you so yearn to bring to fruition in
your life. Pray for healing, for harmonizing all that is
fragmented, within and without.

DAY 28

The Four Winds and the gifts they carry from the Four Realms correspond, in turn, with the Four Rivers: River of Simple Unity *(chee'deh'kel)*, River of Diversity and fruition *(paras)*, River of Belly Flow *(gee'chon)*, and River of Mouth of Transformation *(pee'shon)*. These rivers, in turn, bring us the seasons and their attributes.

DAY 29

From the North flows *chee'deh'kel,* the simple unity we experience happening during winter when everything has become as one, in its emptiness, deathliness, peacefulness; when all has gone below to unify toward future renewal of life above. This is the mystery of water, the element of North. Water resurrects the dormant, the dead, the not-yet-alive, reincarnating or recycling what has gone below, deep into the earth, or what has never before existed, readying it for resurrection or birth in spring by the breath of East.

DAY 30

From the East flows *gee'chon,* the passion we experience
being restored within us and within the earth during spring.
This is when fresh life breath is blowing across the planet to
reawaken all that has lain dormant throughout winter, all that
has been constricted until now by the power of possibility
concealed in the mystery of North. Now they are freed by
the wind of renewal that blows from the East, the place
of Breath.

DAY 31

From the South flows *paras,* the diversity we experience in all the colors and aliveness manifested during summer when the sparks of spring become fanned to full power, blazing into life, aflame with the force of South, heat, and the animating force of its element: Fire.

DAY 32

From the West flows *pee'shon,* the beginning (or mouth) of transformation that we experience during autumn as we glean our produce in our fields, in our actions, and in our hearts. This is a period of introspection, when we start moving inward, leading to personal transformation in the season when everything is changing its color, its texture, its aroma, its dwelling; when everything is moving from tree and brush to earth, like the Jewish people move from house to hut *(sukah)*; when the pine needles fall to the earth to transform the soil around the tree that will eventually restore the sap-flow in midwinter, and the acorns or piñon nuts in summer. This, then, is the season reflective of the element carried by the west: Earth.

DAY 33

Every human should tend very compassionately to the
flesh of their body in order to be able to share with it all the
dimensions of enlightenment and visions of which the soul is
capable, for the body, too, is capable of such perception. Do
not hide your eyes from having mercy upon your flesh, that is
the flesh of your body. You must have much compassion for
your body. See to it that you purify your body so that it can
become conscious of all the enlightenment and visions that
the soul perceives.

—Eighteenth-century RABBI NACHMON of Breslav
in *Likuttei Ha'MaHaRaN* 22:5–7

DAY 34

Darkness is but a garment of light (*Sefer Ha'Zohar*, Vol. 1, folio 22b). It is still light, but veiled; the darker it is the more layers of the veil. Likewise, everything in life is one with its opposite, the extreme of each a veil for the other in varying degrees. If you are feeling anger, know that the anger veils its opposite. Your anger is an extremely thick veil for appeasement, so slowly try to remove the layers until you discover appeasement. If you are feeling hate, remember that hate is a thick layer that veils its opposite, love. But within that very hatred is the possibility of love. And so with everything, all is one. The oneness of all is individuated, but also related one to the other.

DAY 35

They asked Rabbi Tar'fon (first century): If one is thirsty and comes upon water, what prayer ought to be said? He replied: "Source of Blessing are You, Infinite One, Source of our Powers, Council of the Universe, who creates many living beings, each one lacking something unique over all others. By each acquiring what they lack, all other living beings are brought that much closer to fulfilling their own deficiency."

—*Midrash Mechil'ta, B'shalach,* Ch. 5

DAY 36

In the very obstacle that blocks you from discovering God is precisely where God is waiting to be discovered.

—Eighteenth-century Rabbi Nachmon of Breslav
in *Likuttei Ha'MaHaRaN,* No. 115

DAY 37

When you wake up from a bad dream, think positively, find a positive metaphor for the dream and interpret it for the better, because dreams follow their interpretation.

—Third-century RABBI YO'CHANAN
in *Midrash B'reishis Rabbah* 89:8 and *Midrash Eichah Rabbah* 1:18

DAY 38

All of the prophets do not prophesy any time they desire. Rather, they focus their minds and sit in a state of ecstasy and joyful heart, and meditate. For prophecy is not channeled when in a state of sullenness and laziness, only when in a state of joyfulness. Therefore, the disciples of the prophets always have before them stringed instruments—drum, flute, and harp—when they seek prophetic visioning.

—Twelfth-century Rabbi Moshe ibn Maimon
in *Mishnah Torah, Hil'chot Y'sodei HaTorah* 7:4

DAY 39

For a persistent fever, sit on the earth at a crossroads and wait for a large ant to pass by carrying a pebble or a piece of foliage. Take the item from the ant and place it inside a brass container. Shut the container up with lead and seal it with sixty seals. Then shake it, place it on your back, and say: "Your burden be on me and my burden be on you." Another remedy is to take a small fresh jar to a river and say to the river: "River, O river, please loan me a jar full of water for a guest who is visiting me." Fill the jar with water from the river. Then spin the jar seven times around your head and pour the water over your back while saying: "River, O river, please take back the water you gave to me, for the guest who visited me came and left on the same day."

—Babylonian Talmud, *Shabbat* 66b

DAY 40

The snake represents the Trickster, that mysterious force in life that shakes you out of your stupor and gets you moving. Sometimes, the snake tries too hard and tries to overwhelm you with too many life changes all at once. This is where the horn of the ram or antelope comes in handy. Its curves wield the power to transform energies. The smoke of burning grasses or leaves is also potent for bringing balance to extremes. The smoke will bring forth the spirits of the plants and the horn will direct their flow in such a way as to subdue the extremes of either physical or spiritual snake infestation. So, to rid your living space of snakes or your life process of too much trickstering, take the horn of a ram and smudge yourself or the infested physical area with it, having the smoke filter out through the horn.

—*Midrash Tehilim* 22:14

DAY 41

Religion is nice, but even without all that divine revelatory hullabaloo, the Creator left us enough information in the earth about how to live in balance. If we did not have the Torah, we could have learned everything that we needed to know from the animals.

—Babylonian Talmud, *Eruvin* 100b

DAY 42

No less than the Creator teaches us through the Vision Bringers and their scriptures, the Creator also "teaches us through the wildlife of the earth, and makes us wise through the birds of the sky."

—Book of Job 35:11

DAY 43

There is no space void of God's Presence (Isaiah 6:3). What you seek so distant from where you stand is always breathing down your neck (Babylonian Talmud, *B'rachot* 13a). Because everywhere you are, is holy (Exodus 3:5). Likewise, your soul does not live in some hoity-toity part of your body but throughout your being. For as the Creator fills the universe, so does the soul fill the body.

—Babylonian Talmud, *B'rachot* 10a

DAY 44

The soul perceives matters of the Above that the body cannot, and so every person should act with great compassion toward their body so that their soul might inform their body concerning all that she beholds and perceives. And when the body is in this sort of context it becomes wholesome for the soul. For sometimes the soul can fall from her plateau [of spiritual consciousness and graduation], and if the body is clear and illuminated the soul can elevate herself again and become restored to her plateau through the body. Through the pleasures of the physical senses the soul can recall and thus rise again to experience her own delights . . . And also through the impressions of the soul manifested in the body earlier—through the light with which the soul had earlier illuminated the body—she can again recall and rise and return to her plateau. And this is what is meant by "from my flesh shall I behold God" (Job 19:26)—that is, literally through the very flesh of the body shall one behold God, meaning perceptions of the divine, meaning that the human sees and envisions spiritual perceptions by way of the body, for the soul is always visioning.

—Eighteenth-century RABBI NACHMON of Breslav
in *Likuttei Ha'MaHaRaN* 22:5–7

DAY 45

All medicines come from the earth. And therefore, during the time when the earth gives forth her bounty she empowers all trees and plants—especially during the time of her fullness which is in the moon of *iyyar* (around May). Then there is potency in all the medicines, for the earth empowers them. Therefore, one picks the medicinal plants during the moon of *iyyar*. But remember that all plants also share the same divine root. Therefore, if the specifically prescribed herbs are not available or have not been picked in the right moon, one can do as well with any species or during any moon—providing one has faith in the single divine root source of all the forces.

—Eighteenth-century RABBI NACHMON of Breslav in *Likuttei Ha'MaHaRaN,* No. 277, para. 2 and ibid, *Tanina* 1:11

DAY 46

Don't try to figure it out. Let the mystery reveal herself in her own time, at her own pace. Remember always that "there are ten *Sefirot* (ever-spiraling spheres of divine manifestation) without What. Silence your mouth from speaking of it, and your heart from thinking of it. And if your mouth runs to speak it, or your heart runs to think it, return to The Place."

—*Sefer Yetzirah* 1:8

DAY 47

Breath of God is the womb of the initial sphere of Creation in the genesis of its unfolding from primeval thought to eventual realization. This sphere is also known as *Keh'ter*—literally: Crown. Where did you come from? Your origin lies in the primordial thought of the Creator, in the *Keh'ter* realm of the divine spiral that eventually became you becoming you in this very moment. This Primal Thought in the divine mind is manifested as the primeval Light of Genesis, hovering over the cauldron of possibility as Breath, and waiting to spark the spiral of Creation into the dance of manifestation. Breath of God and *Keh'ter* are symbolic of the No-Thing place from where everything originates.

hollow

DAY 48

Wind is the second sphere of Creation spiraling into existence. It is also known as *Choch'mah*—literally: hollowed out. Also: Wisdom. The Creator's Breath of Light became Wind and hollowed out a space in No-Thing in which there now arose the possibility for Some-Thing. This is the beginning of what you experience as wisdom. No wisdom comes to us when we are filled with it. Wisdom only comes when we are void of it, when we have hollowed out a clear space in our selves, and created room for experience and for what experience teaches us. Wind and *Choch'mah* are therefore symbolic of the very initial phase of your genesis from the realm of No-Thing.

DAY 49

Water is the third sphere of Creation spiraling into existence. It is also known as *Bee'nah*—literally: Constructing. Also: Understanding. The first wind built upon the primeval Breath of Light to form vapor that then became Water. Water and *Bee'nah* are then symbolic of the subsequent phase of building upon what you have experienced, building upon the newly evolving premises of the wisdom that is germinating in you. Where *Choch'mah* is the dynamics of hollowing out a space for possibility, *Bee'nah* is the dynamics of creating possibility within that space, and doing so with the very pieces that were chipped away in the process of hollowing it out. Understanding builds on wisdom.

DAY 50

Fire is the fourth sphere of Creation spiraling into existence. It is also known as *Chessed*—literally: Drained. Also: Benevolence. As the moisture of the primeval Breath created water, so did the warmth of the primeval breath create Fire. Fire and *Chessed* are then symbolic of the lovingness that emerges out of the act of creating, of giving form to something, as *Bee'nah* has done to *Choch'mah*. Fire is passion, offspring of the first kiss, of breath and water. The excitement and newness of initial lovingness causes it to flow unconditionally and unbridled, potentially draining *Bee'nah* from the hollow of *Choch'mah,* or drying up the water—reverting everything back to No-Thing.

DAY 51

Sky is the fifth sphere of Creation spiraling into existence. It is also known as *G'vurah*—literally: Powerfulness. Also: Balance. While fire can dry up water and water can absorb fire, the two can also coexist in a fine, fragile harmony and perfect balance in what became Sky. Sky in Hebrew reads as *"sha'mayyim,"* literally "Fire Water," for it is where the two dwell together in balance à la sun and rain. Sky and *G'vurah* are therefore symbolic of the act of balancing the unbridled awkwardness of *Chessed* flow, so that instead of being drained in the act of giving, you are nurtured by it; instead of giving of yourself because it is expected, you give of yourself from a place of strength, and therefore not more than you are capable of giving without being drained. Where *Chessed* is spilling, *G'vurah* is pouring. *G'vurah* provides *Chessed* with a spout, provides randomness with direction, and tempers what would otherwise be running amok.

DAY 52

Earth is the sixth sphere of Creation spiraling into existence. It is also known as *Tif'eret*—literally: Beauty. Also: Pride. Without fire and water, sun and rain, there is no earthly existence. Earth is then brought to her fruition by virtue of sky, by the harmonization of fire and water and the balanced directing of their flows. Earth and *Tif'eret* are then symbolic of your sense of togetherness, your sense of walking your life journey in balance, void of extremes and filled with a sense of accomplishment, or pride. This is the place of the heart, that single organ that centers the rest of our organs, holding it all together as well as sometimes losing it altogether. As the heart sends the life force throughout the body, Earth and *Tif'eret* channel the Divine Light and fan it into a brilliant glow so potent that it shines within you and through you so those around you behold your Beauty. This is good pride, a pride void of egotism since *Tif'eret* leads you on a walk that is far from extremes and always careful and balanced. In *Tif'eret* you become so aware of your strengths and weaknesses that you feel no compulsion to flaunt your strengths and no need to fear your weaknesses. They are both well balanced in a synchronic dance that spins you further and further to the fruition of your deepest essence, the essence concealed in the mystery of the primeval Breath of God.

DAY 53

North Wind is the seventh sphere of Creation spiraling
into existence. It is also known as *Netzach*—literally: Sparked.
Also: Victory and Eternity. As the heart quality of Earth and
Tif'eret sends balance and life force into the four directions
of the body via the four valves of the heart, so too does it
translate the mystery of the primeval Breath of the Creator,
the original spirit wind, into the Four Winds of the physical
realm, causing the primeval wind to blow first from the place
of mystery, or North. North and *Netzach* are symbolic of
asserting your power in all that you do and encounter, being
the one who sparks projects, relationships, or experiences
and sets them ablaze with your presence, and translates your
diverse constitution into a single, powerful force. Some call
this charisma. Some call it intensity. There is probably a
little of both attributes that fuels *Netzach,* a direct flow from
Tif'eret, which has so empowered you that you now come at
everything and everyone from a position of victory, exuding
an air of immortality.

DAY 54

South Wind is the eighth sphere of Creation spiraling into
existence. It is also known as *Ho'd*—literally: Distinction.
Also: Majesty. Everything creates its opposite. The north
wind, too, stirs the creation of the South Wind, whose
warmth tempers the fierceness of the north wind and brings
forth no less power, albeit with gentleness. South and *Ho'd*
are symbolic of what the continuing influence of the nucleus,
the heart, *Tif'eret,* brings to contain North and *Netzach*
within the sphere and dance of balance. You can exert your
power and your presence in a forceful, intimidating way, or
you can exert your power and your presence in a graceful way,
a way in which your power does not intimidate yet comes
across with equal forcefulness. This juggling act requires
being able to distinguish between situations and personalities
that require the more cutting and power-fused *Netzach*
approach, and the more laid-back and majestic *Ho'd*
approach. *Ho'd,* like the balancing arm of *G'vurah,* is situated
on the left side. So, as *G'vurah* tempers *Chessed* to its right,
Ho'd tempers *Netzach* to its right. As *G'vurah* balances out the
overwhelming force of *Chessed, Ho'd* balances out the
overwhelming force of *Netzach.* And *Ho'd,* like *G'vurah,*
determines when it is appropriate to spill in the *Chessed* mode
or to pour in the *G'vurah* mode. *Ho'd* also determines when it
is appropriate to exude in the *Netzach* mode or to simply glow
in the *Ho'd* mode.

DAY 55

East Wind is the ninth sphere of Creation spiraling into existence. It is also known as *Y'sod*—literally: Support. Also: Base, Foundation. The tempering of the extremes between the poles of the north wind and the south wind enables creativity and new beginnings to emerge, and creates the East Wind, or in Hebrew, *keh'dem,* literally: Beginning. East and *Y'sod* are symbolic of the foundation onto which all of the delicately balanced attributes of divine manifestation are fastened, and become the basis for new beginnings. In your physical manifestation, this powerful base is played out or experienced in your sexuality. It is in the act and sensation of sex that you set the stage for new unfoldings. It is during sex that you open up wide the chutes of all of the divine forces. In the crescendo of lovemaking, they channel freely and fully, unleashing all of their powers through you, within you, and out into the universe of your lover, rippling uninterruptedly across the planet and into the cosmos, up through the *Sefirot* and into the No-Thing realm—the very realm of which in that very moment is bringing you and everything in your world into existence.

DAY 56

West Wind is the tenth sphere of Creation spiraling into
existence. It is also known as *Mal'chut*—literally: Council.
Also: Sovereign. Beginnings, like sunrise, flow into motion
toward endings, such as sunset—the direction of the sun's
journey, or *ma'arav* in Hebrew, meaning "the place of
merging." West and *Mal'chut* are symbolic of the bigger
picture that simultaneously emanates from your very being
while encompassing your very being—from the ground you
are standing on to the trees outside your window. *Mal'chut* is
therefore also referred to in the Kabbalah as *Shecheenah,* the
She-Dwelling, or the Divine Presence in Creation, which
is everywhere. So where *Keh'ter* is the Primordial Light,
Mal'chut is the Primordial Prism that gives form to that light,
that draws forth its variety of colors. *Keh'ter* is white light,
containing within it all the colors but in a potential state.
Mal'chut is black, the color of West, containing all the other
colors but in a state of fruition, of climax. West or *Mal'chut*
is where it all ends, and begins. *Mal'chut* brings *Keh'ter* full
circle. Infinity and Divinity are therefore as much in *Mal'chut*
as they are in *Keh'ter.* It is only through the physical translation of spirit, through *Mal'chut,* that we stand any chance
of coming anywhere near Spirit. As is written: "I am the
Infinite One, who [also] dwells deep within the entrails
of the earth" (Exodus 8:22).

DAY 57

All plants, minerals, and animals, including the stars, moons, suns, and planets, are living, conscious beings replete with divine wisdom and soul (Psalms 8:7–8; 145:10; 148:3–4 and 7–11; Isaiah 55:12; Job 12:7–8; *Midrash Heichalot Rabati* 24:3). The second-century Rabbi Me'ir used to call the sun "My brother" (*Midrash B'reishis Rabbah* 92:6).

DAY 58

Ask the animals and they shall teach you;
and the birds of the sky, and they shall inform you.
Or speak to the earth and she shall show you;
and the fishes of the sea shall declare to you.

—Book of Job 12:7–9

DAY 59

The physical reality is seen as an intermediate phase in the ever-spiraling evolution of the fruition of the Creator's imagination or will (*Sefer Ha'Zohar,* Vol. 3, folio 61b). The various phases of this ever-continuing spiral are comprised of myriad *ru'chot,* or "spirits," beings who in turn embody myriad stages involved in manifesting spirit into matter. Every blade of grass, for example, is being constantly invoked into being by a spirit that empowers and influences its growth from within the spiralic process that is, moment to moment, actualizing the seed of divine intention to physical fruition.

—*Midrash B'reishis Rabbah,* Ch. 10;
Sefer Ha'Zohar, Vol. 1, folios 251a and 2:80b

DAY 60

Do you see the magic of this earth? Can you tell it was created with passion? All the colors, the aromas, the scenery, the details . . . Know therefore that when God created, God created with *passion*. "Sacred Wellspring [God] endowed with passion all trees and all grasses that are upon the earth."

—*Sefer Ha'Zohar,* Vol. 1, folio 251a; Isaiah 6:3; Jeremiah 23:24;
Sefer Ha'Bahir, Ch. 10; *Midrash D'varim Rabbah* 2:26

DAY 61

Every human being is comprised of the qualities of every other being on the planet. We are not made solely in the "Image of God" but just as much in the image of all that surrounds us, stones, plants, animals, the galactic beings, as well as in the image of all the chaos and ultimate clarity that went into creating our universe.

—*Midrash HaNe'elam* 1:16b

DAY 62

"The Creator addressed all of creation before making the human, meaning that in creating the human, the Infinite One incorporated all of the attributes of all the animals and plants and minerals and so on that had been created up to this point. In each of us, then, are the powers of all the creatures of the earth."

—Sixteenth-century RABBI MOSHE CORDOVERO
in *Shi'ur HaKomah*, Torah, Ch. 4

DAY 63

Don't feel like something is wrong when you are feeling a little chaotic or confused. You are probably just feeling human. For the human was fashioned "in the image of *Elo'heem*." *Elo'heem* is the God-Name that describes the dynamics of the Creator stirring all of creation into being. It is therefore a plural word connoting "Forces" or "Powers" (*Shulchan Aruch, Orach Chayyim* 5:1). Thus, the human is comprised of the chaotic whirlwind of Primeval Creation, of the divine forces dancing spirit into matter, matter into form, and form into action.

—Eighteenth-century Rabbi Chayyim of Volozhin
in *Nefesh Ha'Chayyim,* Ch. 1

DAY 64

The Four Directions are referred to in ancient Hebrew as
ar'ba ru'chot, or "Four Winds," also Hebrew for "four spirits,"
stressing the organic, living nature of the four directions
(*Sefer Ha'Zohar,* Vol. 4, folio 118b). Each wind or direction
is designated an animal (*Sefer Ha'Zohar,* Vol. 4, folio 18b;
Midrash Bamid'bar Rabbah 2:9): the eagle in the north,
the buffalo in the west, the human in the south, and the
lion in the east.

—Thirteenth-century Rabbi Yitzchak of Acco
in *Sefer M'irat Einayim, Bamidbar,* para. 2

DAY 65

The Fertile Void, as our vast endless universe is called, acts like a prism, translating the single white Light of Creation into myriad colors and possibilities. In our earth, the Light is translated further by the Four Winds: red in the north, black in the west, white in the south, and yellow in the east.

—Eighteenth-century RABBI ELIYAHU of Vilna
on *Sefer Yetzirah,* Ch. 4

DAY 66

The Four Winds are not just breezes or storms blowing at your toupee or at the shingles of your roof. They are an integral part of you. They are living forces, each considered to possess their own distinct power and attribute, all of which are played out in the individual human drama: "The human was created from the powers of the Four Winds."

—*Sefer Ha'Zohar,* Vol. 1, folio 130b

DAY 67

Since you are comprised of all of creation, the animals in your environment mirror important qualities back at you. They are part of what can keep you in balance or throw you out of whack. Live in balance with the creatures of our planet and they in turn will become good medicine for you.

—*Midrash Tana D'bei Eliyahu Rabbah*, Ch. 1

DAY 68

While there are auspicious times during the year when it is best to receive healing plants from the earth, such as in early spring, the Jewish shaman will not take the plant unless the earth is at peace (*Likuttei Ha'MaHaRaN* No. 277), because plants wield great wisdom and powers that are imbued with raw divine energies (*Sefer Ha'Zohar,* Vol. 2, folio 80b).

DAY 69

You are here by default. Yet it would be a good idea to make a conscious commitment to being here, to being in life. The more conscious your commitment to being here, the deeper your soul will manifest in your being. The less the life commitment, the less the soul becomes manifested in the body, and the more vulnerable the body then becomes to death—toward which illness is believed to be a momentum.

—*Likuttei Ha'MaHaRaN* No. 268

DAY 70

If you are feeling sad, look around you at the beings with whom you share this planet. Notice their beauty, their colors, and their aromas. These are their expression of their joy in being. For "All trees rejoice in God's Resonance. And all plants dance in God's Rejoicing."

—*Midrash Heichalot Rabatti* 24:3

DAY 71

When you take your next stroll in the woods, or peer out the window at your lawn, try to hear the chanting that resounds around you. All is singing every moment. "How good and how beautiful is it when one is able to hear the song of the grasses."

—Eighteenth-century RABBI NACHMON of Breslav,
in *Likuttei Ha'MaHaRaN Tanina*, No. 63

DAY 72

Don't forget to kiss the earth for the inspiration she brings to you from without and from within. For all truths emanate from the earth.

—*Sefer Ha'Zohar,* Vol. 3, folio 168a; Psalms 85:12

DAY 73

Lovemaking is far more than sex. It is the kiss of earth and sky, of spirit and matter. For when you make love in earnest, know that you are unifying Creator with Creation, God transcendent with God immanent.

—Babylonian Talmud, *Sotah* 17a and *Ketuvot* 62a

DAY 74

Good and evil are not opposites in conflict but opposites in dance, challenging one another constantly in a concerted dance of divine mystery. For there is no impurity that does not have a kernel of purity, no evil that does not possess a seed with the potential for good.

—*Sefer Yetzirah* 6:4; *Sefer Ha'Zohar,* Vol. 2, folio 69a–b

DAY 75

Everything around you is brimming with aliveness. You are not alone. You are always surrounded by family. "All the trees," taught the ancient rabbis, "converse with one another and with all living beings" (*Midrash B'reishis Rabbah* 13:2). Even the planets and stars have their own songs (*Sefer Ha'Zohar,* Vol. 1, folio 231b).

DAY 76

God loves you. But remember always that God also loves every creation and cherishes every stone, plant, and animal. The ancient rabbis taught that when it rains, it rains not solely for the sake of the human, but that God causes it to rain even for the exclusive sake of a single blade of grass in the far reaches of the earth, far from any human inhabitation.

—Jerusalem Talmud, *Ta'anit* 3:2 and 3; Book of Job 37:13

DAY 77

When King David completed his composition of the Psalms, he bragged to God and said: "Creator of the Universe! Is there any creature in your world that has sung more praises unto your Name than I have?" Suddenly, a frog leaped up on a rock in front of him and croaked: "Don't let it go to your head, for I sing far more praises to God in a single day than you could in a lifetime!"

—*Midrash Yal'kot Shim'oni* on Psalms 150:6

DAY 78

The world you live in and the life you lead can be either Hell or Heaven. It's totally up to you. In first-century Israel, during the violent and oppressive rule of Rome, the Israelites asked Rachumai: "Rabbi, where is Paradise?" He replied: "Here."

—*Sefer Ha'Bahir, Mishnah* 31

DAY 79

What you seek on distant shores is right with you. It is likened unto a king who had seven sons, each positioned behind the other in order of their age, the youngest one stationed in the rear. As the youngest craned his neck in his attempt to see the king, he felt a light tap on his shoulder from behind. He turned around and found the king standing there. The king said: "My son, why do you strain so hard? What do you seek yonder?" The prince said: "I seek your face, my father." The king replied: "But I am right here behind you; you need not strain so to see me."

—*Sefer Ha'Bahir, Mishnah* No. 171

DAY 80

You live in a magical universe. We are taught that the Infinite One hollowed out existence "with thirty-two pathways of wondrous mystery wisdom and then sculpted the universe within three spheres: *sefer, s'por, see'pur*"—[literally: text, number, and story] the universal laws of physics, time and process, and the capacity for free will.

—*Sefer Yetzirah*, Chapter 1, *Mishnah* 1

DAY 81

There are four roads that we walk simultaneously in this life, four dimensions of consciousness. They are: literal experience, allusion to something beyond the literal, the search for meaning, and the road of pure mystery. In their Hebrew original, these four roads make up the acronym that reads PRDS, as in "paradise."

—Babylonian Talmud, *Chaggigah* 14b

DAY 82

Each wind also has a spirit guardian (*Midrash Bamid'bar Rabbah* 2:10) who, when invoked by various Hebrew and Aramaic incantations, brings forth the gift of that particular wind. The attributes of these four spirit guardians are healing, reflection, balance, and vision. The spirit of the north is *Su'gee'el;* the spirit of the east is *Ar'gee'el;* the spirit of the south is *Gar'gee'el;* the spirit of the west is *Mar'gee'el.*

—*Midrash Tal'piee'yot* 121b

DAY 83

Rabbi Shlomo of Karlin (1738–1792) taught that to fully serve God one had to also serve God in the language of all the creations, the grasses, the animals, the trees, and the stones. Rabbi Schneur Zalman of Liadi (1745–1813) mastered the language of the animals.

—MARTIN BUBER's *Tales of the Hasidim* [Schocken Books], Vol. 1, p. 275

DAY 84

You are not an alien to this planet. You are her child. You belong here. Walk on the grass. It's okay. Sit in the mud, it won't hurt you. Accept the cold, the heat, the rain, and the wind. Remember that you are created from the spirit of the Four Winds and from earth taken from all four corners of the planet.

—*Sefer Ha'Zohar,* Vol. 1, folio 130b, and Vol. 2, folios 13a and 23b

DAY 85

The Creator did not say "let there be this or that" six thousand years ago or fifteen billion years ago, but rather *is* saying it right now. Every moment, we are being emanated, willed into existence across the simultaneous stages of unfolding known as the Four Worlds: the world of Primal Thought, the world of Idea, the world of Image, and the world of Happening.

DAY 86

You were made by the one who could make anything happen, even from nothing at all, for the "[Creator] formed substance out of chaos, and made what-was-not into what-is."

—*Sefer Yetzirah,* 2:6

DAY 87

The earth is a living organism. She has feelings, and she reacts. She accepts us or rejects us, depending upon how we conduct ourselves upon her. Even the medicines that come from the earth are capable of healing only when the earth is at peace, not when there is conflict upon her.

—Eighteenth-century Rabbi Nachmon of Breslav
in *Likuttei Ha'MaHaRaN,* No. 277

DAY 88

Every leaf, every stone, is a camouflage of divine mystery. But remember always that the mystery is not only contained in nature, but rather nature herself is part of the mystery.

DAY 89

Were God to cease for a moment to think of you, you would be nonextant in that moment—Woosh! For just as the Sacred Wellspring (God) at the onset of creation brought forth worlds into being from absolutely nothing—likewise from then on, every day and every moment, the whole cause of their existence, arrangement, and being, is dependent solely upon the fact that the Creator is willfully influencing them every single moment with the power to exist and with the nurturance of ever-renewing divine light. And if the Creator were to withhold from them the power of the divine influence even for so much as a fraction of a moment, all would be nothing and desolate.

—Eighteenth-century RABBI CHAYYIM of Volozhin
in *Nefesh Ha'Chayyim*, 1:2, para. 1

DAY 90

This mysterious Void Place is also known in Jewish mystical tradition as *teheru* (*Sefer Ha'Zohar,* Vol. 2, folio 277a), a space in nonspace that is both void of God and yet filled with God. If *teheru* was only filled with God, then nothing but God could exist, and if it was only void of God, then, too, could nothing exist. So it is both void and filled, in the sense that it is just sufficiently void of God in order to allow for the possibility of existence, and just sufficiently filled with God in order to allow for the happening of existence. Thus, God is at the same time hidden and revealed.

—*Sefer Ha'Zohar,* Vol. 1, folio 39b

DAY 91

A message from God: "You wish to know my name?
According to the nature of my actions am I called. At times I
am called *eyl shadai,* or *tz'vaot,* or *Elo'heem*. When I judge the
creations, I am called *Elo'heem;* when I battle wrongness, I
am called *tz'vaot;* when I suspend the sins of humanity, I am
called *eyl shadai;* and when I exercise compassion upon my
worlds, I am called *yhwh*. In other words, I was what I was, I
am what I am, and I will be what I will be—for I am known
by various names, each according to the nature of my action
in the moment."

—*Midrash Sh'mot Rabbah* 3:6

DAY 92

Don't think you can peg God down, figure God out, or profile God. "The Self-Essence of the Blessed Endless One is hidden beyond all that is hidden, and we must not—Heaven forbid!—purport to describe this Self-Essence even with the Tetragrammaton, and even with the most core component of the most divine of names. That which is comprehended somewhat by us, and we decorate this grasping with various God-Names and Divine Attributes and the like—as we find in our scriptures and in the various forms of our prayers—reflect only God's relationship with the universes, and the causative powers of Creation with which they are continuously imbued from the time Creation first began. And even [in invoking] the essential, singular name *yhwh* itself we are not connecting with the Selfhood-Essence of God but with that aspect of the Blessing Source that is in relationship with the universes [as their Creator], as the name itself connotes: "The One Who Was, Is, Will Be, and *Is'es* All"—meaning that the Sacred Wellspring is engaged willfully and intentionally with the universes to *Is* them and to maintain their existence every moment.

—Eighteenth-century RABBI CHAYYIM of Volozhin
in *Nefesh Ha'Chayyim* 2:2, para. 2

DAY 93

When you experience good stuff in life, be thankful for the blessings bestowed upon you by the Creator but don't get stuck with any emotional IOUs. Your credit with God is good and unlimited. Just say thank you and don't try to bless God back. Learn to receive. Learn to feel worthy of what God gives you; learn to feel deserving. "The matter of reciting a blessing implies in no way a blessing-praise of God's Selfhood-Essence—Heaven forbid! Heaven forbid!—for God is far above any blessing-praise possible."

—Eighteenth-century Rabbi Chayyim of Volozhin
in *Nefesh Ha'Chayyim* 2:2, para. 2

DAY 94

The notion of blessing God is at least as preposterous as offering a trillionaire a postdated check for half a cent. Rather, and in the context of the theology that composed the prayer, the meaning is not "Blessed art thou . . ." but more like: "Source of Blessing are You, the One Who Was, Is, Will Be, and who *Is-es* all existence, Who . . ." Blessing prayers are acknowledgments, not IOUs. Prayer itself is a kind of welcoming of the Creator's Will to be in relationship with Creation. The more that Will is invited, the more vivid the experience of that presence in our lives.

—*Sefer Ha'Zohar,* Vol. 2, folio 135b

DAY 95

Reciting a blessing over an apple you're about to eat can be a mere "thanks" or it can be a powerful incantation to draw forth the blessing of food to the planet from the Source of Blessing. "The blessing-prayer implies dependence of the universes upon the Blessing Source Who seeks relationship with the universes. Indeed, had the Blessing Source not shown us that it is the divine will to be in relationship with the universes, it would be inappropriate for us to pray to God altogether since prayer assumes that God is in relationship with the universes and involved in the affairs of Creation. Proclaiming God as the 'Source of Blessing' is then intended to call upon the manifestation of the dynamics of the Creator's relationship with Creation."

—Eighteenth-century RABBI CHAYYIM of Volozhin
in *Nefesh Ha'Chayyim* 2:3, para. 3 and 2:4, para. 1

DAY 96

Sacred tasks and shamanic rites are performed only after reciting an invocation of one's intention to unify the Creator with Creation (*l'sheym yee-chud kud'sha b'reech hu u'shecheentey ahl y'dey ha-hu bid'chilu ur'cheemu l'yacheyd shem yud-hey b'vav-hey bee'ychuda sh'lim tah-mir v'ne-elam*)—"For the sake of unifying the Sacred Wellspring with the *Shecheenah* (the divine feminine presence in the earth), through this act, performed in awe and in love, to unify the name *yh* in *wh* in a total union, veiled and concealed."

—Sixteenth-century Rabbi Yeshayahu ben Avraham
in *Sh'nai Luchot HaB'rit, Sha'ar HaOti'ot,
Ot Aleph, Emet V'Emunah*, No. 18

DAY 97

They asked Hillel the Elder (first century B.C.E.): "Where are you going?" He replied: "I am going to perform a sacred deed." They asked: "And what is this sacred deed of Hillel?" He said: "I am going to the House of the Chair (i.e., the toilet)." They asked: "But is that a sacred thing to do?" He said: "Yes indeed, for by so doing one prevents the body from deteriorating." Another time they asked him: "Where are you going?" He replied: "I am going to perform a sacred deed." They asked: "And what is the sacred deed of Hillel this time?" He replied: "I am going to the bath house." They asked: "Is that a sacred thing to do?" He said: "Yes indeed, for by so doing one cleanses the body. Know that the statues of Caesar that are erected in the arenas are but facsimiles of the Image of God, yet the Romans wash them daily. If that which is but a facsimile of the divine image is deserving of such honors, so much more so is the body, which was actually created in the Image of God."

—Babylonian Talmud, *Avot D'Rebbe Natan* [version 2],
end of Ch. 30

DAY 98

Physical desire is an important component of spiritual evolution. In fact, it is a prerequisite. "Without the desires of the physical senses we have as much chance at spiritual enlightenment as a mule does at becoming pregnant."

—Thirteenth-century RABBI YITZCHAK of Acco,
Quoted in *Rei'Sheet Choch'mah, Sha'ar Ha'Ahavah*, Ch. 4, end

DAY 99

Any semblance of the absence of God is due only to the density of the layers of physical garb camouflaging the Divine Presence in that person, place, or situation. The more dense the garb with which the Divine Presence is concealed due to the profane nature of the circumstance, the more difficult it becomes to experience the presence of the divine in that moment or place. But the more one draws close to the Spirit, graduating from level to level in bettering themselves, the clearer their experience of the Divine Presence. The density of the garb then gradually begins to thin so that one will then experience pure love of self and of the Creator.

—Eighteenth-century RABBI NACHMON of Breslav
in *Likuttei Ha'MaHaRaN* 33:2

DAY 100

Prayer is a kind of welcoming of the Creator's Will to be in relationship with Creation. The more that Will is invited, the more vivid the experience of God's presence in our lives.

—Eighteenth-century Rabbi Chayyim of Volozhin
in *Nefesh Ha'Chayyim* 2:2, para. 2

DAY 101

"Praise the Creator, O sun and moon, all you stars of light, you skies above the skies, you waters above the heavens; and praise the Creator from the earth, all you sea monsters and all creatures of the deep; fire, hail, snow, and vapor, stormy winds fulfilling Its word; mountains and hills, fruit trees and all cedars; beasts, cattle, creeping-crawlies, and winged beings . . . all of them praise the Infinite One."

—Book of Psalms 148:3–4

DAY 102

The bird that just excreted on your windshield is not just a fellow creature of the earth. Her soul and your soul are kin. There is a part of you in her, and a part of her in you. For "the souls of animals are sparks of human souls."

—Thirteenth-century Rabbi Shlomo ibn Aderet
in *Manuscript Parma—de Rossi 1221,* folio 288b

DAY 103

You can learn a lot about yourself by communing with the animals. You can also learn a lot about animals through understanding yourself. Because each of you carries the understanding of the mystery of the other. As the ancient rabbis taught: "The souls of animals and humans are imprinted on each other."

—*Sefer Ha'Zohar,* Vol. 1, folio 20b

DAY 104

Each of us, taught the second-century Rabbi Yo'sei the Galilean, walks this earth endowed with the powers and attributes of all creations, of every horse, of every leaf, of every rock; of both spirit and matter, of sky and land, even of wind and water.

—Babylonian Talmud, *Avot D'Rebbe Natan,* end of chapter 31

DAY 105

When your mind feels clogged, or when you feel stuck
in your process, do something that will bring you joy, for
joyfulness frees up the mind, as is written: "With gladness
shall you go out" (Isaiah 55:12)—that through joy you are
made free and can go out from whatever is keeping you stuck.
And if you cannot find the means to gladden your heart, think
about something positive about yourself and it will bring
you to joy.

—Eighteenth-century RABBI NACHMON of Breslav,
in *Likuttei Ha'MaHaRaN Tanina*, No. 10

DAY 106

Every single wisdom in the world has a particular chant, a particular melody. And when you chant that specific melody it will draw forth the particular wisdom to which it is attached.

—Eighteenth-century RABBI NACHMON of Breslav
in *Likuttei Ha'MaHaRaN,* Ch. 60, No. 4

DAY 107

In the future, we will have to account before the Creator for all the pleasures that we wanted to enjoy, were permitted to enjoy, and had the opportunity to enjoy, but didn't.

—Third-century RABBI ZECHARIAH
in Jerusalem Talmud, *Kidushin,* end of chapter 4

DAY 108

Natural is an excuse to not explore any further. After all, it's natural.

DAY 109

While you walk the earth in animation be aware that you are
being formed, and that your formation is being created, and
that your creation is being emanated. At your very root, then,
you are simply a thought. You're not as sophisticated as you
believe, and not nearly as complicated as your therapist
suggested. You are a thought. A figment of God's
imagination.

DAY 110

We exist in four realms simultaneously. All four are simultaneous phases, yet each is a translation of the other. As you are reading this, in other words, you are being thought, willed into existence, and hollowed out, carved, sculpted, stirred, animated, and moved.

DAY 111

You are creation in process, a flower unfolding, a seed sprouting. You are a living paradox of No-Thing and Some-Thing, of "what" and "without what." This consciousness is known as the Sacred Walk: "Walk before me and be *tamim* [literally, both simple and whole]" (Book of Genesis 17:1).

DAY 112

Wind should not freeze you. It should enliven you even more, for "All of the Four Winds join together to form the singular spirit that animates all of creation."

—*Sefer Ha'Zohar,* Vol. 1, folio 235a and 239a,
based on Book of Ezekiel, Ch. 37:9

DAY 113

When you hear the raven caw, have your umbrella handy, for the heavens are about to open their chutes and pour upon you blessings galore. As the ancient rabbis taught: "When the raven calls out, rain is sent to the world."

—*Midrash Pirkei D'Rebbe Eliezer,* end of Ch. 21

DAY 114

How righteous you are is not determined by how holy you
think you are by virtue of your religious observance but by
how you live with others, how you relate to other creatures,
and how deeply you endeavor to understand them. As the
tenth-century B.C.E. King Solomon taught: "The righteous
person knows the soul of their animal."

—Book of Proverbs 12:10

DAY 115

Rabbi Yisro'el Ba'al Shem Tov (1700–1760) taught that the Divine Presence dwells in the life of all four beings, the Still Beings (stones, planets), the Sprouting Beings (grasses, trees), the Living Beings (animals, fish, insects, birds), and the Talking Beings (humans). "She is inherent in all creatures of the universe, whether they are good or bad."

—*Tol'dot Yaakov Yosef,* p. 25

DAY 116

Rabbi Dov Baer of Mezeritch (1698–1772) spent a great chunk of his time meditating around ponds in order to learn the songs of the frogs. Rabbi Pinchas of Koritz (1728–1790) taught the languages of birds, animals, and plants.

—MARTIN BUBER's *Tales of the Hasidim* [Schocken Books], Vol. 1, pp. 266 and 111

DAY 117

"All of nature is but the external garment of God." Keep it clean and nicely ironed. Treat all creations with respect. Nature is God's fashion statement. She has good taste. Try to model yourself after her.

—Eighteenth-century Rabbi Schneur Zalman of Liadi
in *Tan'ya*, Ch. 42

DAY 118

Rabbi Z'ev Wolf of Zbarascz (early nineteenth century) was a Horse Whisperer: "You must never whip a horse," he admonished, "you just have to know how to talk to them."

—MARTIN BUBER'S *Tales of the Hasidim* [Schocken Books], Vol. 1, p. 160

DAY 119

"You find that when the Holy Blessed One desired to create the primeval human, she consulted the ministering angels and said to them: "Should we make the human?" They said: "What is the human that you even bother thinking about them?" (Psalms 8:5). The Creator replied: "The human that I wish to create, its wisdom is superior to yours." What did the Creator then do? She gathered all of the animals, wildlife, and birds and stood them before the angels, and said: "Okay, assign them names." The angels just stood there and didn't know what to call them. She then brought all of them to the primeval human and said to it: "What are the names of these?" The human said: "Master of all the universes! It is fitting to call this one buffalo, and to this one it is fitting to call lion, and to this one horse, and to that one camel, and to the other one eagle," and so with all the other animals. The Creator said: "And what about you? What shall be your name?" The human said: "Earth Being *(Ahdam),* because I was created from the earth *(Ahdamah)*."

—*Midrash Kohelet Rabbah* 7:32

DAY 120

I shall arrange praises day and night
Unto you, Source of Powers, who created all beings,
Holy guardian-spirits and the children of humans,
Animals of the wilderness and birds of sky.

—From a Sabbath hymn by sixteenth-century
RABBI YISRO'EL BEN MOSHE of Najara

DAY 121

Desperation often weakens our grasp. When you grab for a lot, you come away with nothing (Babylonian Talmud, *Chaggigah* 17a). Rabbi Yehudah of India (third century) said: "Once we were on a ship and we saw in the waters a sea serpent wrapped around a precious stone. When a diver attempted to fetch the stone, the serpent rose from out of the waters and tried to swallow the entire ship. But then along came a raven and bit off the serpent's head and the waters turned to blood. Immediately, a second serpent appeared, seized the precious stone, suspended it over the dead serpent, and resurrected it. The first serpent tried again to swallow the ship when along came another bird, bit off its head, grabbed the precious stone, and threw it onto the ship. At the time, we had a supply of salted birds aboard the ship for our food supply. As soon as the stone touched the dead birds, they were restored to life, seized the stone, and flew away."

—Babylonian Talmud, *Baba Bat'ra* 74b

DAY 122

The ancestors are giants. There is much to learn from them, but don't get stuck in the past—for you, too, are an ancestor. Rabbah Bar Bar Channah said: "Once I was journeying in the desert when I came upon an Arabian traveler. As we walked together, he kept picking up sand, sniffing it, and directing me this way and that, promising that it would lead to water. When he wasn't looking I picked up some sand from a different place and put it in front of him but he wasn't fooled. At one point, he informed me he knew where the ancient Israelites lay, the ones that died during the Exodus journey. I begged him to show me. He brought me to where they lay. They were so huge that we were able to walk beneath the thighs of those whose legs were propped. I cut a snippet of cloth from one of their garments to take with me as a souvenir when suddenly we were unable to budge. The Arabian turned to me and said: "You must have taken something from this site, for we have a tradition that anyone who removes anything from this place will be unable to leave." I put the piece of cloth on the ground and we were freed to continue our journey.

—Babylonian Talmud, *Baba Bat'ra* 73b–74a

DAY 123

Sometimes all hell breaks loose in the world, and we are left with shattered hopes, broken faith, doubt, and burning questions. Miraculously, though, the stench of tragedy eventually dissipates and life goes on. The ancient teachers put it this way: "When Leviathan is hungry, it emits a fiery fire from its breath that boils the waters of the deep. Were it not that Leviathan sticks its head into the Garden of Eden, no one could survive the stench of its breath."

—Babylonian Talmud, *Baba Bat'ra* 75a

DAY 124

Every part of you is filled with the very mystery whose
unraveling you seek. We are taught that there are thirty-two
paths through which we attain mystery wisdom. The mystery
enters us through the space between our skull and our spine.
And from there it spreads throughout the body into our
senses. [Twenty digits, four palms, two eyes, two nostrils,
two ears, one mouth, and the heart. The numerical value
of the Hebrew word for "heart," *lev,* is 32.]

—Eighteenth-century Rabbi Eliyahu of Vilna
in his commentary on *Sefer Yetzirah* 1:2, Note 5

DAY 125

There are three Mothers. They are a great and wondrous mystery, a mystery that is concealed and sealed with six rings. And from them emanate Fire and Water, and split into masculine and feminine. There are three Mothers. Air, Water, and Fire are their foundation in the Spirit Realm. And from them were born the Fathers, who manifested them into the realm of the physical and from whom, in turn, all was created. There are three Mothers, Air, Water, and Fire. The skies were created first, from Fire. Earth was created from Water. And Air mediates between the Fire and the Water.

—*Sefer Yetzirah,* 3:2 [and commentary of twelfthth-century Rabbi Avraham ibn Daud]

DAY 126

In the second century, Rabbi Yo'sei taught: It is written: "Open for me, my sister, my beloved friend, my perfect dove . . ." (Song of Songs 5:2). Thus does the Sacred Wellspring say to us: "Open for me as wide as the eye of a needle, and I in turn shall open for you a passageway so wide that entire caravans of tents and wagons can pass through it with the greatest of ease."

—*Midrash Pesik'ta D'Rav Kahana,* folio 163b [in the Buber Edition]

DAY 127

There are a number of different ways of believing. There is a faith, for example, that is solely in the heart. But the main principle is that a person's faith ought to be so great that it fills the *entire* body. As is written in the teachings of Rabbi Yitzchak Luria (sixteenth century), one should raise the hands with palms facing the head following the ritual of washing the hands before bread. This, he taught, is in order to channel the holy. So you see how one needs to have one's faith not only in one's heart but also in one's *hands!*—one needs to believe that by raising one's hands with palms facing the head, one channels holiness. As is written about Moses when he raised his hands to bring victory to his warriors: "And his hands became faith" (Exodus 17:12).

—Eighteenth-century RABBI NACHMON of Breslav
in *Likuttei Ha'MaHaRaN,* No. 9

DAY 128

With the annual changes in the seasons of various plants
of the earth and their time of fruition, there are also born
changes in the soul of all creatures. Thus, living creatures born
in one particular year are not akin to living creatures born in a
different year. And you're not the same in winter as you are in
autumn. Mood changes are often as natural an occurrence as
are seasonal changes.

—Twelfth-century Rabbi Avraham ibn Daud on *Sefer Yetzirah,* 3:4

DAY 129

Air, Water, and Fire actually constitute a great and powerful name of the Blessing Source (God), and with it one can, through its pronunciation, walk safely upon fire. (Don't try this at home.)

—Tenth-century Rabbi Sa'ad'ya Ga'on on *Sefer Yetzirah,* 3:2

DAY 130

Every animal, beast, bird, and creeping-crawly is empowered
by a spirit. These spirits are keepers of great mystery. Therefore, through the chirp of a bird, for example, or the sound
of any animal, one can also discover great mystery concealed
therein by virtue of their life force emanating from one of
those spirits. For those very spirits, keepers of the mysteries,
will at times filter some of those mysteries through the
sounds made by the animals they empower.

—Sixteenth-century RABBI CHAYYIM VITAL of Calibrese
in *Sefer Ru'ach Ha'Kodesh, D'rush Gimmel*

DAY 131

Although the air of the earthly atmosphere is thick in volume and mass, the mystery wisdom of the spirit realm still manages to enter this world because of the birds. For when the birds are in flight, their flapping wings cut through the thickness of the atmosphere, enabling in that moment for the mystery wisdom of the spirit realm to come through to our world. And this is what Solomon (tenth century, B.C.E.) taught: "For the birds of the sky shall enable the Voice to journey" (Eccl. 10:20), referring to the voice of mystery wisdom emanating from the spirits who influence the animals. And there are other birds whose chirping mingles with the sounds of their spirits. About this, Solomon wrote: "and a winged creature shall communicate a word" (Eccl. 10:20). However, there are also birds who communicate the mysteries not through their speech, but through the sound of their wings when in flight.

—Sixteenth-century RABBI CHAYYIM VITAL of Calibrese
in *Sefer Ru'ach Ha'Kodesh, D'rush Gimmel*

DAY 132

Next time a mosquito's hum or a fly's buzz annoys you, recall this Kabbalistic teaching: "Even worms, flies, and mosquitoes, all of them communicate wisdom, and there is not a single animal in the world, even from amongst the creeping-crawlies, that does not communicate some form of wisdom."

—Sixteenth-century RABBI CHAYYIM VITAL of Calibrese
in *Sefer Ru'ach Ha'Kodesh, D'rush Gimmel*

DAY 133

The heavens respond best when there is passion on the earth,
for that passion then rises to the heavens like sacred smoke
and arouses the desire of the heavens to respond with rain.
This is akin to the feminine, which is the earth, rousing the
desires of the masculine, which is the sky. The sky then
responds by bringing down the rains and impregnating
the earth so that she might birth forth her children.

—*Sefer Ha'Zohar,* Vol. 1, folios 29b, 35a, and 46a-b

DAY 134

Sometimes you really really feel the presence of God in the world, and in your life. And sometimes, you have trouble accessing that sense of Divine Presence. Rabbi Zalman Schachter-Shalomi calls God "The Great Cosmic Flasher." More ancient rabbis put it this way: "The Sacred Wellspring (God) is both revealed and concealed." God is always present, and at times that presence is conspicuous, and at times mysterious. But never absent.

—*Sefer Ha'Zohar,* Vol. 1, folio 39b

DAY 135

There are seven realms in the earth, each with their own attribute: *Ahdamah* wields peace, *teh'vel* wields bounty, *gey'a* wields power, *yabashah* wields potential, *eretz* wields wisdom, *ar'ka* wields love, *char'vah* wields life.

—OTZAR HASHEM on *Sefer Yetzirah* 4:4

DAY 136

Every person on the earth has a double, a spirit-self that, unlike the spirit beings and angels, has no permanent existence in its own right but flourishes as long as it does only by virtue of the earthly body with which it is clothed in the physical realm. And when a person is asleep, their spirit-self separates from this earthly garment and journeys to the heavenly realm where it is consumed by the Consuming Fire [God (Deuteronomy 4:24)] who then resurrects it anew and restores it to its earthly garment, the body. This is the intention behind the words of the prophet Jeremiah: "God renews them every morning; how magnanimous is God's graciousness" (Lamentations 3:23); that the human is created anew every single day, and that is no small matter.

—*Sefer Ha'Zohar,* Vol. 1, folios 19a–b

DAY 137

Rabbi Yo'sei opened his teaching with the following: "The greatest secret of all secrets is that the universe was not created before [God] first raised a single stone. This stone is called the Stone of Nurturance, and the Sacred Wellspring [God] lifted it up and flung it into the Abyss. It drifted from above to below, and from this stone did the entire universe emerge. This stone is the center, the very dot of primeval beginning of the universe. This stone is made of fire, spirit, and water. All three of these forces combine and become therefrom a single stone, established over the Abyss. And at times, this stone oozes forth waters that then fill the Abyss. And from this stone, in turn, all of the universe is blessed."

—*Sefer Ha'Zohar,* Vol. 1, folio 231a

DAY 138

If you'd like to participate in the cosmic symphony, you can start by saying a prayer when you wake up in the morning, as the ancient rabbis taught: "In the third part of the night, the stars and constellations break out in song. When you chant your prayer in the morning, you continue their song into the day."

—*Sefer Ha'Zohar,* Vol. 1, folio 231b

DAY 139

The act of picking grasses and herbs for healing use is a
sacred act. Like prayer, it must not be interrupted, because
it requires full concentration and total dedication of
consciousness.

—*Sefer Ha'Zohar,* Vol. 2, folio 80a

DAY 140

Rabbi Shim'on bar Yo'chai (second century) said: "Come and see, that there is not a single blade of grass that is born of the earth that does not draw enormous wisdom from the heavens and enormous power from the heavens."

—*Sefer Ha'Zohar,* Vol. 2, folio 80b

DAY 141

Once, Rabbi Shim'on bar Yo'chai was sitting at the entrance to the village of Lod when he noticed that the sun was darkening, then illuminating, darkening, then illuminating, three times. He lifted his eyes toward the sun and noticed that it shone with the colors black and green. Turning to his son Rabbi El'azar, he said: "Come, my son, let us go and find out what terrible fate has been decreed upon this place, for this is a sign that something ominous is about to happen in the world." As they walked through the field, they came upon a snake slithering along the earth, its mouth wide open, its tongue wagging, and consuming the dust of the earth as it moved. Rabbi Shim'on approached it and tapped the snake on the head. The snake stopped in its tracks, ceased movement of its tongue, and shut its mouth. Rabbi Shim'on said: "Snake, snake, go and say to the Great Snake of the Upper World that Rabbi Shim'on son of Yo'chai is still here on the earth!" The snake slithered toward an adjacent hole and disappeared into it. Rabbi Shim'on said: "I hereby decree that just as the snake of the Lower World has returned into the cavity of the earth, so shall the Snake of the Upper World return to the chasm of the Great Abyss." Rabbi Shim'on then began to pray. While they were praying they heard a heavenly voice proclaim: "Return to your homes, for the harm that was forthcoming will not reach the earth, because Rabbi Shim'on bar Yo'chai has annulled it."

—*Sefer Ha'Zohar,* Vol. 3, folio 15a

DAY 142

Rabbi Tanchum bar Chiyyah (second century) said: "Greater than the Revelation to our people at Sinai is the falling of the rains. For the Revelation at Sinai was to a single people, in a single period of history, on a single mountain; whereas the falling of rain is [a Revelation] to all peoples, in all times, in all places, and to all animals and wildlife and birds."

—*Midrash Tehilim* 117:1

DAY 143

"The world was created with ten utterances. But could God not have created her with a single utterance? Rather, it is to teach you how precious the earth is, and how much reward for those who cherish her and how great the consequences for those who abuse her."

—Babylonian Talmud, *Avot* 5:1

DAY 144

Rabbi Avahu (third century) asked: "What blessing ought one to recite for rainfall?" Rabbi Yehudah replied in the name of Rav: "One ought to say, 'We acknowledge before you, Infinite One, Source of our Powers, our gratefulness for each and every drop of rain that you have brought down to us.'"

—Babylonian Talmud, *Ta'anit* 6b

DAY 145

Our spirit is comprised of water and fire. The water aspect of our spirit settles in the consciousness and draws the divine flux from above, as water moves from above downward. The fire aspect of our spirit settles in the heart and draws the divine flux upward from below, as fire is fueled from below and drawn from above. The breath/spirit itself settles in the two wings of the lung.

—*Sefer Ha'Zohar,* Vol. 4, folios 227b

DAY 146

In each and every organ of the body are waves of the Spirit
Realm (water) and the Physical Realm (fire). The two are
constantly flowing upward and downward, the water downward, the fire upward. The spirit dwells between the two
realms, and its vessel is the earth. For she, the earth, is the
Shecheenah, the feminine manifestation of the Divine
Presence.

—*Sefer Ha'Zohar,* Vol. 4, folios 227b–228a

DAY 147

Just as birds in flight must open their wings to receive wind in order to fly, all the organs of the body must likewise open to receive the spirit through many orifices, many pores, many passageways, the many chambers of the heart, and the chambers of the mind. For if the spirit—which harmonizes the upper and lower realms—would not fill the chambers of the heart, the fire of the heart would consume the entire body. It is no wonder, then, that there are a number of passageways and vents between the heart (fire) and the lungs (spirit), all of which maintain proper balance.

—*Sefer Ha'Zohar,* Vol. 4, folio 227b

DAY 148

Before one begins to speak, the waters of consciousness flow
down upon the wings of the lung and awaken sound. The
sound then rises through the rising fire of the heart to
become speech, carried by the warm breath of the mouth.

—*Sefer Ha'Zohar,* Vol. 4, folio 227b

DAY 149

Corresponding to the two wings of the lung that open to receive wind, are the two lips of the mouth that then take the emerging sound and cause it to fly upward as speech. And corresponding to the five branches of the lung [segmental bronchi] are the five avenues of pronunciation: guttural, labial, palatal, lingual, and dental.

—*Sefer Ha'Zohar,* Vol. 4, folio 227b

DAY 150

The soul manifests in the body as a flock of birds. Each bird perches on a particular limb and organ of the body. Nestled upon each and every branch of the body, for they are the branches of the Tree, these birds sing the life force into manifestation within every limb and organ, filling them with divine light through every manner of song.

—*Sefer Ha'Zohar,* Vol. 4, folio 228a

DAY 151

So long as the petals of the rose are folded shut, she has
no aroma and does not rise above the thorns. But when she
opens her petals, she gives forth aroma and stands out above
the thorns. Likewise, so long as our hearts are closed and we
are not open to turning our lives around, our auras lack luster,
and we fade into oblivion. But when we unlock our hearts and
open ourselves up to turning our lives around, we sparkle,
and we rise above the mediocre and transcend painfulness.

—*Sefer Ha'Zohar,* Vol. 4, folio 232b

DAY 152

There are many graduating realms of spiritual evolution for the righteous individuals in this world. The highest of them all is Love. And therein dwells God, who is always enrobed in Love. And God never ever separates Itself from Love. As is written: "And a river flows forth from Eden" (Genesis 2:10). Indeed, it flows forth continuously, and bonds with the universe in Love.

—*Sefer Ha'Zohar,* Vol. 5, folio 267b

DAY 153

Beginning is the ultimate, singular unity that is not revealed, and through which the Unknowable Infinite One created two hidden universes. And with what were these two universes formed? With that single concealed point called Beginning, that is Wisdom, about which it is written: "You created all through Wisdom" (Psalms 104:24). And these two universes did not become revealed until the Unknowable Infinite One clothed them in two garments. And what are these two garments? The heavens and the earth.

—*Tikkunei Ha'Zohar*, folio 63b

DAY 154

The heavens are the garb of the transcendent universe,
created through the transcendental point of Beginning;
the earth is the garb of the corporeal universe, created
through *Elo'heem*—she is the Great Mother. The *Y* of *YaH*
is Beginning, that is Father of all; the *H* of *YaH* is *Elo'heem*,
that is Mother of all, Mother of all Living. And Wisdom,
he is Father, and cannot be known except through
Understanding, she is *Elo'heem*. Thus *YaH* is the divine
name combining Father and Mother as one, two
universes concealed in mystery.

—*Tikkunei Ha'Zohar,* folio 63b

DAY 155

The soul is manifested in the persona as *ne'shamah*, Life Breath, that is the consciousness; *ru'ach*, Spirit Wind, that is the emotion; and *nefesh*, Body Integration, that is the appetitive. The three manifestations of Soul enliven the persona like fire illuminates a lamp. *Nefesh* is the wick, *ru'ach* the oil, and *ne'shamah* the flame. As is written: "For the Life Breath of the human is a flame of the Infinite One, searching throughout all the chambers of the belly" (Proverbs 20:27).

—Tikkunei Ha'Zohar, folio 14b

DAY 156

One time, Rabbi Shim'on bar Yo'chai (second century) noticed that the earth had darkened and become filled with gloominess. He turned to his son Rabbi El'azar and said: "Come and let us see what God has in store for the world." They went, and came upon an angel the size of a great mountain, with three flaming torches emanating from its mouth. Rabbi Shim'on said to it: "What have you come to do to the world?" Replied the angel: "I have come to destroy the world." Rabbi Shim'on said: "I conjure you to go to God and tell God that the son of Yo'chai is still on the earth." The angel went to God and repeated the words of Rabbi Shim'on. God said to the angel: "Go back and destroy the world, and pay no attention to the son of Yo'chai." When the angel returned, Rabbi Shim'on approached once more and admonished the spirit: "If you will not go away, I will utter an incantation upon you that will prevent you from ever again returning to the heavens! And you will end up like the fallen angels Aza and Aza'el. Therefore, return and tell God that if the world is destined for destruction because there is no majority of good people here, there is myself and my son. And even if only I alone am worthy, is it not written: 'And the righteous person is the foundation of the world' (Proverbs 10:25)?" In that instant, a voice emanated from the Heavens and declared: "How worthy is your portion, Rabbi Shim'on, in that God decrees above and you abolish the decree below?"

—*Tikkunei Ha'Zohar,* folios 255a–b

DAY 157

All four earth beings (mineral, plant, animal, and human) are willed into existence by the Creator through four circles, one circle within the other. Each being possesses its own soul and that of the soul it encircles. The stone has a mineral soul. The sprouting beings possess both their own soul as well as that of the stone. You see this in actuality, that when a sprouting being withers, its soul leaves and yet the soul of the mineral being remains within it, transforming it into stone as in petrified wood, or into earth. The animal beings possess their own soul as well as the soul of the plant and the mineral. The human is comprised of the souls of all three.

—*Pit'chey Sh'arim* 10a

DAY 158

The sacredness of the circle is that it symbolizes the grace of the Creator. The circle has no left side or right side, no part that is bigger or smaller, or less important or more important than any other. Likewise the Creator's nurturing and willing of Creation into being is not discriminating between good people or bad people, a blade of grass, or an elephant. All of creation is nurtured and willed into existence with equal lovingness of the Creator; all receives equal blessing from the divine flow that, like the circle, knows no sides.

—Pit'chey Sh'arim 10a

DAY 159

The sages of our time are dominated by their wives because these holy men are the reincarnated souls of the generation of the Exodus—specifically of those who did not try and stop the dissidents from making the golden calf. However, the women of that time declined complicity and refused to surrender their jewelry to the golden calf builders (*Midrash Pirkei D'Rebbe Eliezer,* Ch. 45). Therefore, these women now dominate their husbands.

—Sixteenth-century RABBI CHAYYIM VITAL
of Calibrese in *Sha'ar Ha'Gil'gulim,* Intro. 20, para. 5

DAY 160

In an instance where a woman is infertile, she might possibly be the reincarnation of a man. And if a male healer succeeds in interceding on her behalf and reversing her barrenness, he might possibly be a reincarnation of a woman, for he wields the powers of conception and birthing.

—Sixteenth-century RABBI SHMU'EL VITAL
in *Sha'ar Ha'Gil'gulim,* middle of Intro. 36, note 6

DAY 161

Every moment is a new beginning; every act your very first. Never regard your action as if it were the second or fourth or hundredth, but always as if it were the very first time you've ever done it.

—Eighteenth-century Rabbi Nachmon of Breslav
in *Likuttei Ha'MaHaRaN,* Ch. 62:5-6

DAY 162

You can be healed from anything, even bread and water. Know that for every illness there is a particular grass that can heal it, sometimes situated in far reaches of the earth and which potency is only available in spring. Yet, if the grass for your particular illness is not immediately available, know that you can be healed from anything, even bread and water, for all share the same common heavenly root; all emanates from the Creator who wills everything into existence. Thus, if you cannot access the medium, turn to the root cause of all causes; pray to God and your prayers will in turn channel the flux of healing from the one root of all in the heavens through whatever is available to you on Earth. For the healing benefits of herbs for specific ailments is a reality only in the physical realm, because the root of all healing comes from the Creator.

—Eighteenth-century RABBI NACHMON of Breslav
in *Likuttei Ha'MaHaRaN Tanina,* Ch. 1:9–11

DAY 163

When you pray in the field, all the grasses merge within your prayers and support you and empower your prayers. And if you cannot pray in the field, but only in your house, then even a bowl of fruit or vegetables can help as well since they are of the earth. Only, it is more potent when you pray in the field.

—Eighteenth-century RABBI NACHMON of Breslav
in *Likuttei Ha'MaHaRaN Tanina,* Ch. 11

DAY 164

No space is void of the Divine Presence, as is written: "The entire earth is filled with its glory" (Isaiah 6:3). As our sages taught us: "God fills all of the universes and surrounds all of the universes." No one, regardless of who they are or what they do, can claim that they are void of God's presence. Because, as our sages taught, one can find a spark of the divine in all and in everything, for without the Divine Presence nothing can exist.

—Eighteenth-century RABBI NACHMON of Breslav
in *Likuttei Ha'MaHaRaN* 33:2

DAY 165

When one focuses one's mind on something, even on money, it will manifest. But one must concentrate only through the mind, not through any of the senses of the body. The mind is so powerful that one can even approach the brink of death by meditating on dying to the point that the thought brings on the actual experience of dying. Therefore, while it is helpful to do this meditation as a means of being prepared for a necessary situation of martyrdom, one should be cautious not to remain in that state for too long lest one actually dies prematurely, God forbid.

—Eighteenth-century Rabbi Nachmon of Breslav
in *Likuttei Ha'MaHaRaN,* Ch. 193

DAY 166

When you encounter an obstacle to your journey toward God, know that God is hiding within the obstacle waiting for you. As is written: "And Moses drew near to the dark cloud wherein was God" (Exodus 20:18), meaning he drew near directly into the obstacle, for therein was God hidden.

—Eighteenth-century Rabbi Nachmon of Breslav in *Likuttei Ha'MaHaRaN*, Ch. 115

DAY 167

Rabbi Abba (second century) was walking along the road with his son Rabbi Yitzchak. They came upon some roses. Rabbi Abba picked one of the roses and they continued to walk. As they were walking they encountered Rabbi Yo'sei. Rabbi Yo'sei said to them: "I see with certainty that the *Shecheenah* (feminine presence of the divine) is here. And I see her in the hand of Rabbi Abba, imparting great wisdom. For I know that Rabbi Abba did not pick that rose but for the sake of learning the wisdom that she carries." Rabbi Abba replied: "Sit, my sons, sit." They sat down upon the earth. Rabbi Abba inhaled the scent of the rose and declared: "It is without doubt impossible for the world to exist without aroma. And we see indeed how no soul can survive without aroma."

—*Sefer Ha'Zohar,* Vol. 1, folio 20a

DAY 168

In order to serve God, one must have access to the enjoyment of nature, so that one might sit and meditate in view of flower-decorated meadows, majestic mountains, flowing rivers, and so on. For all these are essential for the spiritual development of even the holiest of persons.

—Twelfth-century Rabbi Avraham ben Ha'Rambam
in *Ha'Maspik L'Avodat Hashem,* p. 165

DAY 169

Leadership has little to do with academic achievement and more to do with how conscientiously you direct your life. Rabbi Yo'sei (second century) said: "Every moment a sheepherder conscientiously applies his skill toward guiding his sheep, he becomes the more ripe for divine appointment as a spiritual leader."

—*Sefer Ha'Zohar,* Vol. 2, folio 20b

DAY 170

All beings—all of them—are interconnected one within the other, and support one another, and it is impossible for any one of them to *exist* without the other. Likewise, there are wondrous medicines in all of the four *merka'vot* (vehicles of divine manifestation)—Still Beings, Sprouting Beings, Wildlife Beings, and Talking Beings.

—Sixteenth-century RABBI YESHAYAHU BEN AVRAHAM
in *Sh'lah ahl M'sechet Yoma,*
Perek Derech Chayyim V'tocha'chat Musar, No. 29

DAY 171

To go into a trance that will bring you knowledge and vision of things you've never known or seen before, you will need to drum, and you will need musical accompaniment. As is written: "And it will happen that when you arrive at the village, you will encounter a group of Vision-Bringers descending from the Sacred Space, and before them are the stringed instrument, the drum, the flute, and the harp. And they are visioning."

—Hebrew Scriptures, First Book of Samuel 10:5

DAY 172

When you pray, direct your eyes toward the earth and your heart toward the heavens. For the Creator dwells everywhere, no less in the earthly realm than in the heavenly realm.

—Babylonian Talmud, *Yevamot* 105b

DAY 173

Rabbi Pinchas ben Ya'ir (second century) was on his way to the House of Study, his disciples following behind him, when they came to a raging river. He said to the river: "What are you accomplishing by preventing me from proceeding to the House of Study?" The waters withdrew and he passed over the river safely. When he reached the other side, his disciples shouted to him: "Master, may we, too, cross over?" He shouted back: "Any amongst you who has never insulted another creature may cross over without danger."

—Jerusalem Talmud, *D'mai* 1:3

DAY 174

Rabbi Pinchas ben Ya'ir (second century) approached a village when the inhabitants surrounded him and complained how the mice had been infesting their crops. He conjured the mice to appear before him and "spoke" to them in their language, and they "spoke" back to him. He then turned to the crowd and asked: "Do you understand what these mice are saying?" They said: "No, master." He replied: "They claim that your crops have not been shared with the poor." They said: "Swear to us that this is so, and that the mice will vanish if we share our crops with the poor." He swore to them. They corrected the situation and the mice never returned.

—Jerusalem Talmud, *D'mai* 1:3

DAY 175

There are forty-nine gates of defilement and forty-nine levels of degradation of how low a person can fall. Yet, the fiftieth and ultimate gate is the holiest of them all, for at that level there exists no duality, only goodness and wholeness. Because on that very plane dwells the Root Source of all Unity.

—*S'fat E'met,* p. 181

DAY 176

All trees communicate with one another. All trees converse
with all living beings. It happened that a man tore up his
orchard, when a fierce wind came and wounded him.

—*Midrash B'reishis Rabbah* 13:2

DAY 177

God says: "I am the Infinite One who dwells deep within the bowels of the earth; the earth belongs to me, and you are but temporary residents with me."

—Hebrew Scriptures,
Books of Exodus 8:18; Leviticus 25:23; Psalms 24:1

DAY 178

It is already established knowledge that all that exists Below
spirals into manifestation from Above, spiral upon spiral.
And behold, the existence of the Below is Still Being (stones),
Sprouting Being (plants), Life Being (animals), and Speaking
Being (human), and these correspond with the four basic
elements of Earth, Water, Fire, and Air. Still Being emanates
from the element Earth, and Sprouting Being emanates from
the element Water, since it is the rainfall that moisturizes
the land that births and sprouts forth vegetation. Life Being
emanates from the element of Air, and is described as "all
that has in it the Living Spirit" (Genesis 6:17), and if not for
that Living Spirit, which is of the element Air, it would die.
Speaking Being is the human, whose distinctiveness is by
virtue of its Soul Breath (Genesis 2:7), which emanates
from the element of Fire Spirit, as is written: "a flame of
the Infinite One is the Soul Breath of the human"
(Proverbs 20:27).

—Sixteenth-century Rabbi Yeshayahu ben Avraham in *Sh'lah ahl
Sefer Vayik'ra, Perek Torah Ohr M'Sefer Torat Kohanim,* Ch. 4

DAY 179

It is known that the four elements are rooted Above and above the Above, for they emanate from higher than the highest down to the four realms of the *Shecheenah* (feminine manifestation of the divine): *Meecha'el, Gav'ree'el, Uree'el,* and *Refa'el. Meecha'el* is the base source of Spirit Water, *Gav'ree'el* of Spirit Fire, *Uree'el* of Spirit Air, *Refa'el* of Spirit Earth. And these four spirit elements spiral forth in turn from four other base sources, each of which is progressively higher and more spirit than the next. They are the four Upper Life Beings: lion, buffalo, human, and eagle.

—Sixteenth-century Rabbi Yeshayahu ben Avraham
in *Sh'lah ahl Sefer Vayik'ra,*
Perek Torah Ohr M'Sefer Torat Kohanim, Ch. 4

DAY 180

The Realm of Emanation is the abode of the four letters of
the divine name *YHWH* that constitute the root of the root
of the roots of the four elements. *Y* being the primal root of
Water, *H* being the primal root of Fire, *W* being the primal
root of Air, and the second *H* being the primal root of Earth,
as is known to the Sages of Truth. Within each of these
planes exist tens of thousands of further planes without
measure, until all that exists returns [is traced] to its single
hidden Root. Then shall you understand that the Infinite
One is the Source of All the Forces in the sky above and in
the earth below, and that there is no other. This means that
nothing exists whose existence is external to God, for
everything is from God, blessed be.

—Sixteenth-century RABBI YESHAYAHU BEN AVRAHAM
in *Sh'lah ahl Sefer Vayik'ra,*
Perek Torah Ohr M'Sefer Torat Kohanim, Ch. 4

DAY 181

There is nothing from the Other [Evil] Side that does not retain within it a spark of the Divine Light. All things cleave to one another, both the pure and the impure. There is no purity except through impurity, thus from good can come evil, and from mercy can come cruelty. All are intertwined, the impulse for good as well as the impulse for evil, as each is interdependent upon the other.

—*Sefer Ha'Zohar,* Vol. 2, folios 69a–b, and Vol. 3, folio 80b

DAY 182

Why is there so much rivalry and competition amongst friends and relatives? Because it is possible that they share the same Root Soul from which each reincarnated a particular, unrealized attribute for the purpose of actualizing it in this lifetime. If they only knew that their bickering is a result of each of their soul's competing with the other in suckling from their common Root Soul, they would love one another and not be in conflict.

—Sixteenth-century Rabbi Chayyim Vital of Calibrese
in *Sha'ar Ha'Gil'gulim,* Intro. 20, para. 6

DAY 183

Chant rises from a person's deep internal desire for connection with the Creator. Thus, the more potent the chant, the more it testifies to the authenticity of the spiritual grade that has been achieved by the one intoning the chant.

—Sixteenth-century RABBI YEHUDAH LOEW of Prague
in *Kitvei Maharal M'Prag,* Vol. 2, p. 356

DAY 184

One can measure a person's degree of cruelty toward people by measuring the degree of their cruelty toward animals.

—Sixteenth-century Rabbi Yehudah Loew of Prague
in *Kitvei Maharal M'Prag*, Vol. 2, p. 360

DAY 185

The injunction that you ought not to hate others includes not creating cause for others to hate you.

—Sixteenth-century RABBI YEHUDAH LOEW of Prague
in *Kitvei Maharal M'Prag,* Vol. 2, p. 360

DAY 186

Through chanting, you can lift up the souls who are stuck in the Fertile Void, the *chalal ha'p'nu'yah*.

—Eighteenth-century RABBI NACHMON of Breslav in *Likuttei Ha'MaHaRaN*, Ch. 60, No. 4

DAY 187

Before you come into this world, you already know all that there is to know (*Sefer Ha'Zohar,* Vol. 3, folio 61b). In the womb, you are shown from one end of the universe to the other, and taught the highest of mystery wisdom. Then, when you emerge into the light of this world, when your soul becomes in that moment manifested in your body, all is forgotten (Babylonian Talmud, *Nidah* 30b). Why is this? Why bother knowing before birth what you will inevitably forget after birth? For it is as if the soul is a sculptor and the body a sculpture in progress. And while the artisan retains the end result of the intended image, this knowing will not become realized through the art itself until it has been successfully completed and refined. Likewise, it is our soul-self that is informed of all wisdom prior to our birth, and then, once we are born, endeavors to imbue our persona with that knowledge. This is a task that takes many years, and the quality of which depends upon the clarity of body and mind to receive what is being channeled from the soul.

—Seventeenth-century Rabbi Menashe ben Yisra'el
in *Nish'mat Chayyim,* Treatise 2, Chapter 10

DAY 188

Mother of the Above Realms is called Friend, because the love of God that flows through her streams unceasingly to all the universes. Mother of the Below Realms is called Bride, and also Sister, for she is inseparable and intimately connected to all.

—*Sefer Ha'Zohar*, Vol. 3, folios 77b–78a

DAY 189

To read the scriptures literally is akin to telling someone that they are a magnificent cloak, as if the person is nothing more than what they wear. Certainly a body exists behind the cloak, and certainly a soul behind the body. Likewise, it is with the sacred scriptures. The narratives they contain are like garments to yet a far more precious body. In turn, this body is a garb to yet a far more precious soul, and within that soul yet another and another. Why, if there is nothing to the scriptural writ other than their text, I myself could have composed a far superior literature.

—Second-century RABBI SHIM'ON BAR YO'CHAI
in *Sefer Ha'Zohar,* Vol. 3, folio 152a

DAY 190

Once there was a man who grew up isolated in the mountains and had never laid eyes upon another human. His primary sustenance was wheat and he knew only raw wheat. One day, he came upon a village and noticed the people of the village were eating strange foods. He inquired of one woman, "What are you eating?" She said: "I am eating bread." He asked: "What is it made from?" She said: "It is made from wheat." The man approached a second villager and asked: "What are you eating?" He said: "I am eating cake." The man of the wilderness said: "And what is it made of?" He replied: "It is made from wheat." And so it happened that as he went inquiring from person to person, each one dining on a substance of a different shape and texture, whatever they ate was made from wheat. Finally, he declared to the villagers: "I am far superior to all of you; for I eat wheat itself, while you eat foods derived thereof." He returned to the wilds, only to spend the rest of his life missing out on, and unaware of, the pleasures of the world in all of their varieties.

—*Sefer Ha'Zohar*, Vol. 2, folios 176a–b; *Sif'ra D'Tzni'uta*, Ch. 1

DAY 191

When you become inspired toward divine service, this desire flows first to the heart, to the very foundation and mainstay of the entire body. And thereafter, this goodwill filters through the heart to all of the organs and limbs of the body. Then, the will of all the limbs and organs of the body join with the will of the heart, and together they draw upon themselves the illumination of the *Shecheenah* (the feminine attribute of the Divine Presence) who then dwells with you. And in that moment, you become merged with God.

—*Sefer Ha'Zohar,* Vol. 2, folio 198

DAY 192

The more challenging the obstacle that you face in life, the more spiritually evolved you will become if you prevail over it. Because it is about effort, not achievement (first-century Rabbi Ben Hay'hay in Babylonian Talmud, *Avot* 5:26). As the ancient Kabbalists put it: "There is no light as brilliant as that light which manages to emerge from out of the darkness."

—*Sefer Ha'Zohar,* Vol. 1, folio 32a and Vol. 3, folio 47b.

DAY 193

In the moment when the Cherubim lift up their wings from Below to Above, letters fly from above and below, and they meet each other in flight. They then merge together and kiss one another with the kiss of Love until all the universes become one and the Sacred Wellspring becomes one—a total union that is without any separateness whatsoever.

—*Zohar Chadash* 63:4

DAY 194

All kisses that are inspired by love wield the power to join the two in total oneness without any quality of separateness. These kinds of kisses merge one with the other, merge universes with universes, forging all diversity into total unity, so that all becomes one.

—Zohar Chadash 63:4

DAY 195

Rabbi Zechar'yah said: "The place of the entire universe is but a single point, upon which all stands." What is this point? It is the point of Primeval Thought, the original thought of the Creator concerning the creation. It is concealed within this point, awaiting translation, waiting to be drawn out, and to be drawn in one direction or another. And this point is the very beginning of all will and of all thought in the entire universe. And the more it draws forth, the more is revealed of all that is concealed within the point. But not completely, only as much as a whisper. Analogous to a line starting forward from a point, a dot. The line is the beginning of the revelation of the unknown thought concealed within the point, in the thought of the artist or the writer, but it reveals only a direction of movement, not the entire mystery of the emerging thought behind it.

—*Zohar Chadash* 71:2

DAY 196

When two lovers kiss one another on the mouth, they exchange four breaths: each takes in the breath of the other and gives the other their own breath. The four breaths then join to become a single breath, that is the breath of the child born onto them. As is written: "And a single breath shall appear from out of the Four Winds" (Ezekiel 37:9).

—*Zohar Chadash* 60:3

DAY 197

Why is woman called *ee'shah*? From the word *esh*, fire. The *h* at the end of *ee'shah* is one of the sacred letters of the ineffable God-Name *yhwh*, for woman is Divine Fire. Fire can consume; fire can create. Thus, woman dances the two into balance, harmonizing the divine force of judgment with the divine force of compassion.

—*Sefer Ha'Zohar,* Vol. 4, folio 259b

DAY 198

Do not suppose that God sends only messengers that are filled with the Breath of Life. Even objects that are not filled with the Breath of Life can be sent to us with a message from God. Come and see how even the dead, dried-up branch that was the staff of Aaron, the brother of Moses, was chosen by God to carry out the first miracle on behalf of the Israelites in Egypt. It swallowed the serpents that had come out of the staffs of Pharaoh's magicians, and later it sprouted fresh leaves as a sign to authenticate Aaron's position as High Priest. Thus, in the very moment of its mission, a lifeless stick was granted the Breath of Life.

—*Sefer Ha'Zohar,* Vol. 2, folios 25b

DAY 199

It is written: "And God said, 'Let us make Human in our image, according to our Likeness'" (Genesis 1:26)—"In our Image," that is Light; "According to our Likeness," that is Darkness, for Darkness is the garment of the Light no less than the body is the garment of the soul.

—*Sefer Ha'Zohar,* Vol. 1, folio 22b

DAY 200

Rabbi Yehudah (second century) was on his way out of his home one day when he discovered Rabbi Yitzchak sitting outside his door, his countenance sullen. Rabbi Yehudah asked him: "What is different about this day from yesterday?" Rabbi Yitzchak replied: "I have come to request of you three things—when you teach, memorialize my name by crediting to me any of the teachings that were mine, teach my son Yo'sef, and visit my grave every day of the seven days of mourning and pray for me." Rabbi Yehudah said: "And what makes you think you're about to die?" He replied: "Lately, when my soul leaves my body during sleep, she shows me no dreams. Also, when I pray, I notice the absence of my shadow." Rabbi Yehudah said: "All that you have requested, I shall fulfill. But one thing I request of you. When you reach the Other World, reserve a space for me beside you just as I have been with you in this world." Rabbi Yitzchak wept and said: "Please do not leave my side during the days to come." They went to Rabbi Shim'on bar Yo'chai, who was meditating. Rabbi Shim'on lifted his head and saw the Angel of Death dancing around Rabbi Yitzchak. Rabbi Shim'on said: "Let only those enter my chamber who are accustomed to visiting me." The Angel of Death stopped at his door and did not enter. Rabbi Shim'on then took Rabbi Yitzchak's hand and asked: "Have you ever seen a vision of your deceased father? For we have a tradition that when one is about to die their family and close friends come to them to greet them and to usher them to their designated place in the Other World." Rabbi Yitzchak said: "I have never seen such a vision." Rabbi Shim'on turned to his son Rabbi El'azar and said: "Take his hand and hold it." He took his hand. Rabbi Shim'on began to meditate and Rabbi Yitzchak fell into a deep sleep. In his sleep his father appeared to him and informed him of the bliss that awaits him in the Other World. Rabbi Yitzchak then asked him: "Father, please inform me of the day that I am to die." His father said: "I am not permitted to reveal such things. All I am allowed to say is that when you come to the Other World, you will be seated at the table of your master Rabbi Shim'on." Rabbi Yitzchak awoke in a state of joy and remained in gladness the rest of his days.

—*Sefer Ha'Zohar,* Vol. 1, folios 217b–218a

DAY 201

The lights emanating from the stars are created by virtue of their song. When the stars sing, they glow. Therefore, when you gaze at the stars, know that they reveal themselves through their song. Thus, when you rise in the morning to pray, know that your prayer is a continuation of their song.

—*Sefer Ha'Zohar*, Vol. 1, folio 231b

DAY 202

All is intertwined one with the other, purity with impurity, for there is no purity except through impurity. And this mystery is alluded to in the Sacred Writ: "Who can give forth purity from impurity, if not the One?" (Job 14:4).

—*Sefer Ha'Zohar,* Vol. 2, folio 69b

DAY 203

Rabbi Yannai (second century) said: "What did Moses see that led him to the Burning Bush? He saw birds spreading their wings and flying toward the area but not venturing into the area." Rabbi Yitzchak said: "He saw them flying away from there and falling at his feet. He then sensed something special was going on there, and so he left his herd and entered into the area alone."

—Sefer Ha'Zohar, Vol. 2, folio 21a

DAY 204

Rabbi Shim'on bar Yo'chai (second century) was engaged in a shamanic journey at the shore of the Mediterranean, when the ancient prophet Elijah appeared to him in a vision. Elijah said: "What is the meaning of the verse, 'Lift up your eyes to the heavens and see who created these (Isaiah 40:26)'?" Rabbi Shim'on said: "It means one should appreciate the wonders of the skies, the stars, the planets." Elijah said: "I shall reveal to you a great mystery. When the Hidden of all Hidden chose to create existence, that moment of choosing became the very beginning of the possibility for existence to come into being. And within that choice was carved and hollowed the image of how the universe was to unfold, how it was all to be shaped. So when you look up into the vast sky, know that you are in that moment looking into the eye of the primeval thought, the primordial choice for all existence to unfold."

—*Sefer Ha'Zohar,* Vol. 1, folios 1b–2a

DAY 205

Looking for a good book? Try the universe. It comes complete with commentaries. As the eighteenth-century Rabbi Tzadok HaKohain put it: "The universe is God's book; Divine Inspiration its commentary."

—*Sefer Tzid'kat HaTzadik,* No. 219

DAY 206

It is preferable that meat be consumed only by the spiritually evolved (Babylonian Talmud, *P'sachim* 49b). For it may be that the reincarnated soul of a fellow human is clothed in the soul of the animal we are eating, waiting to be graduated into human carnation, as is taught in the school of Rabbi Yitzchak Luria (*Sha'ar Ha'Gil'gulim,* Ch. 22, para. 6).

—Eighteenth-century RABBI TZADOK HAKOHAIN
in *Sefer Tzid'kat HaTzadik,* No. 240

DAY 207

Just as it is important for you to believe in God, so is it important for you to believe in yourself.

—Eighteenth-century Rabbi Tzadok HaKohain
in *Sefer Tzid'kat HaTzadik,* No. 154

DAY 208

Moments in your life when you feel distant from God and feel absent of any desire for the sacred are actually moments in which you are being readied for magnanimous spiritual epiphanies.

—Eighteenth-century RABBI TZADOK HAKOHAIN
in *Sefer Tzid'kat HaTzadik,* No. 151

DAY 209

If you are feeling overwhelmed by lust, do not despair, for—
on the contrary—the greater the intensity of your lust, the
greater the potential of your passion for Love and Truth.

—Eighteenth-century RABBI TZADOK HAKOHAIN
in *Sefer Tzid'kat HaTzadik,* No. 44

DAY 210

The highest degree of prophecy is not when one hears God speaking to them in actual physical speech. That would be a far lower degree of prophetic experience designated for someone who would not otherwise be capable of receiving divine communication. For divine communication emanates from the mind of God, filtering through all the phases of soul consciousness until it resonates within the very persona of the recipient who must then translate spirit resonance into physical verbiage. The more direct experience of God actually speaking words in the physical sense is therefore known as *baht-kol,* literally: "Daughter of the Voice," meaning a secondary, indirect experience of the actual communication from God.

—Sixteenth-century Rabbi Moshe Cordovero
in *Sheey'ur Ko'mah,* Ch. 32

DAY 211

The way of the Kabbalist is to always go off on the tangent while teaching. Do not be puzzled if I begin with a particular subject and speak of it briefly, and then, just as what I am revealing to you becomes clear to you, I dance to something else, related in theme but distant in relevance to the subject I started out with. This manner of teaching is consonant with how one should be exploring mystery wisdom to begin with, as is written: "And the Life Forces were flying to and fro, to and fro" (Ezekiel 1:14).

—Twelfth-century Rabbi Avraham Abulafia
in *Sefer Ha'Chey'shek* 3:6

DAY 212

Most of our yearnings, as they bring us to aliveness also culminate in deadness, as with honey and wine. The more the honey, the less the effect of the wine; the more the wine, the less effect of the honey. To keep the yearning alive it must not be climaxed, not be allowed to settle in resolution but always kept dynamic. So the teacher is busy supporting, nurturing, and enhancing those who are hungry and thirsty for wisdom until their yearning is sated, and they are strengthened and replenished. In the process, however, the teacher grows weaker and weaker, and is drained of all energy, and must return to the place of potential for the restoration of energy and power. And so it continues, to and fro, to and fro, as the Spirit Beings are portrayed in the vision of Ezekiel (1:14). The teacher must dance from potential to realization and back again, to and fro, to and fro. Thus, all that is in the potential state is being drawn to the realized state and from realized back to potential from whence it drew its inspiration. Thus, there is no creative yearning without a subsequent art, and there is no art save that which the artist derives from inspiration. So all that lives is art, and all that is art lives.

—Twelfth-century Rabbi Avraham Abulafia
in *Sefer Ha'Chey'shek* 3:6

DAY 213

Every individual must find their own relationship with the Creator, as is written: "Do not make with me gods of gold and gods of silver. An altar of earth shall you make for me"— meaning, God does not want us to follow blindly in the footsteps of our teachers and parents when it comes to relating with the divine. Rather, we are each asked to find our own individual way; we are each asked to build "an altar of earth," implying a quality of simplicity from which any variety of possibilities can sprout from our own personal truths.

—Eighteenth-century Rabbi Mordechai Yosef of Ischbitz
in *Sefer Mei Ha'Shi'lo'ach*, Vol. 2, folio 16b

DAY 214

Just as God fills the entire universe, the soul fills the entire body. Just as God sees but cannot be seen, the soul sees but cannot be seen. Just as God sustains the entire universe, the soul sustains the entire body. Just as God is pure, the soul is pure. Just as God dwells within the chamber of chambers, the soul dwells within the chamber of chambers. Let she who possesses these five qualities come and praise the One who also possesses these same five qualities.

—Babylonian Talmud, *B'rachot* 81a

DAY 215

Nothing is more important than peace. Without peace
and cooperation, nothing can exist. If one of the stones of
a building decided it wanted to move to the top rather than
remain in the middle or at the bottom, the entire structure
would collapse. If the root of a tree chose to emerge atop the
soil, the tree would die. If one of our hands decided not to
cooperate with the other, we could not build anything, nor
could we eat. If our legs tired of being apart all the time and
chose to unite, we would fall. All exists by cooperation, by
each valuing their respective contribution to life, and each
honoring the preciousness of the other.

—Seventeenth-century RABBI ELIYAHU HA'ITAM'RI
in *Shey'vet Mussar*, Ch. 37

DAY 216

Reincarnation goes something like this: If I were to leave this lifetime never having tasted a good knish, some part of me would feel a knish-void once I've left the physical world, and would yearn to come back and haunt some deli, either as a *dybbuk* or as a *nudnik*. A *dybbuk* is a soul that refuses to leave the physical world because it feels a knish-void. And so it roams the planet looking for some hapless *schmeggeg* who is also looking for a good knish—and then possesses that person. Maybe together they stand a better chance of finding the right deli. A *nudnik* is the one who's running amok with a compulsive lifetime obsession with the Search for the Holy Knish. *Nudniks* and *dybbuks* attract one another. And to some extent, we all go through life possessing a little of both these qualities.

DAY 217

Even after thousands of years of discovery and wonder about nature, neither has been exhausted. There will always be more to uncover, more left to wonderment. As Rabbi Abraham Joshua Heschel put it: "It is within man's power to seek [God]; it is not within his power to find Him."

—*God in Search of Man,* p. 147

DAY 218

The shaman in the Judaic tradition does not rush into a
spiritual experience like a famished desert traveler arriving at
an oasis. Moses is not desperate for a vision because he knows
that looking for one often gets in the way of seeing one. When
we put all our energies into seeking we risk not finding, we
risk rushing right past it. "If you grab for a lot, you've come
away with nothing."

—Babylonian Talmud, *Er'chin* 4b

DAY 219

The Hebrew word for the physical universe is *o'lam,* which also means "hidden" because the universe hides the Creator (Jeremiah 23:24; *Sefer Ha'Bahir* 10; *Midrash D'varim Rabbah* 2:26) who can be discovered in the marvels of the universe. Therefore, God is only sought, not found, because the wonders of Creation can never be fathomed in a single lifetime.

DAY 220

To turn your enemy into a friend, do the following. Before
the sun rises, go to the outskirts of the village and station
yourself facing the direction from which the sun is rising.
And in the moment that you see the appearance of the circle
of the sun, recite: "I wish to greet you in peace from the
Sacred Wellspring of all, Who created me and Who created
you. And I request of you that you be a messenger to so-and-
so to stir in them love toward me. And as you warm up the
mountains and the hills, likewise please also warm up the
blood and flesh of this person so that they may love me
always with a love that is brazen and solid. So may it be."

—*Ha'rofey Ham'nuseh* 30:4

DAY 221

If you experience fear while walking on a long journey, do the following. Gather seven small stones from along the path on which you are traveling. As you gather them, recite: "Infinite One is the Source of all the Powers, the True Living Cause of all Forces and Council of the Universe, in whose annoyance the earth trembles, and from whose displeasure the nations shy away" (Jeremiah 10:10). Then take four of the stones and throw one toward the east while calling out the name *Ar'gee'el;* throw a second stone toward the West while calling out the name *Mar'gee'el;* throw a third stone toward the South while calling out the name *Gar'gee'el;* and throw the fourth stone toward the north while calling out the name *Su'gee'el.* Bind the three remaining stones in a corner of your garment and resume on your journey in peace. And if you experience any sense of terror along the way, remove the bundle of the remaining stones from your garment and hold them in your hand.

—*Midrash Tal'piee'yot* 121b

DAY 222

Let me explain what Hell is. It is not literally a furnace of fire, for after all, how can fire burn a soul? A soul is in itself a fire more fierce than any flame, more potent than any heat, whether physical or spiritual. No, Hell is not literally any form of fire or heat that burns and scorches the soul. Hell is the experience of the soul when it leaves the body and in that moment becomes fully aware of what it had neglected to realize here on earth. It is also fully aware of what it had neglected to realize of its spiritual self while incarnated in this world of action. If I do not know the Spirit while here, and only obsess with the Body alone, then, when I leave my body, my soul will pine for what it no longer possesses the means to experience, this earthly life. And so it will also pine for what it is incapable of experiencing, the spiritual life, having never availed itself of that experience while "alive." This agony of soul is what we call Hell. Eventually, the soul adjusts to the Light from which it had chosen to be estranged, and eventually is embraced by the blissful experience of basking in that Light.

—Fourteenth-century RABBI YOSEF AL'BO
in *Sefer Ha'Ikkarim* 4:33

DAY 223

You might think, "Of what worth is my doing good works in the world? I have accomplished so little in the realm of the sacred, so what is the point of trying to do any more than what little I've done? I may as well throw all caution to the wind." But my friend, that is akin to discovering a hole in your pocket and that all of your money, except for one coin, has fallen through and been lost. Would you then use this same logic and throw away the one remaining coin as well? On the contrary, what little you've done is perhaps the greatest thing you will ever have done; it counts. And it should encourage you to continue to do more good works, for every minute act of goodness is far greater than you can imagine.

—Seventeenth-century Rabbi Eliyahu Ha'Itam'ri
in *Shey'vet Mussar,* Ch. 45

DAY 224

The stars in the sky visible to the eye, are but fruits of the seeds the Creator first planted at the time of Creation. They are fruits born of stars that cannot be seen, stars that were seeded in the Field of Stars in the Upper Realm.

—Twelfth-century Rabbi Yitzchak Saggei-Na'hor
on *Sefer Yetzirah,* Ch. 4

DAY 225

To discover the meaning of a dream, go out on the first day of the week to the seashore or to the river bank in the third hour of the night, and garb yourself in a new blanket. Do not eat any fish nor anything of blood, and do not drink any wine. And take some fresh myrrh and frankincense and smoke them upon some stones in a new bronze basin. Then incline your face toward the water and call out the names of the sky and water spirits until you see a column of fire appear between Sky and Earth. Then say the following: "I ask of you in the name of the one who made spirits to fly in the air, ministering before her as burning fire, and who dries up the sea and turns rivers into desert; in her name and in the letters of that name and in the name of the spirits of the seventh sky—*O'ru'dee, Garee'b'el, Put'mus, Sar'ga'ree, T'lee'gos,* and *Asaf'du'fa'rus*—I ask that you inform me of the meaning of the following dream . . ." And do this also on the second day and the third day, and you will see that amid the column of fire and mist upon the water there will appear the image of a person. Bring your quest to her and she will tell you all that you desire. If you wish to release the vision, take some water from the sea or the river and cast it to the sky and say under your tongue: "In the name of *O'ru'dee, Garee'b'el, Put'mus, Sar'ga'ree, T'lee'gos, Asaf'du'fa'rus*—I hereby release you, I hereby release you. Remove yourself and return to your path." Say this seven times. You will perform this in purity of intention and you will succeed.

—*Sefer Ha'Razeem,* end of Ch. 1: *Ha'Ra'kee'a Ha'Rishon*

DAY 226

Clowning around is no joke. It is actually an important component to achieving true wisdom. There is indeed no wisdom as clear and as deep as the wisdom that was achieved through jesting, for humor opens the heart and mind so that wisdom can be absorbed more wholly. Therefore, the masters would always begin their teachings with jesting.

—*Sefer Ha'Zohar* Vol. 3, folio 47b

DAY 227

Don't take the burdens of the world's problems upon yourself.
Don't ignore them, either. As Rabbi Tar'fon (first century)
put it: "The work is not upon you to complete, but neither
are you exempt from trying."

—Babylonian Talmud, *Avot* 2:21

DAY 228

The Blessing Flow from Above comes to us in strengths and quantities commensurate with our desires and efforts to draw it Below. This is akin to breast milk, abundant and ready to flow forth, but dependent upon how determined the infant is in suckling. Likewise, if we are not actively drawing from the Blessing Flow, we receive but little drips from it. Whereas if we open our hearts fully with determination and faith, we receive the blessings in ample quantity.

—*Kitsur Sefer Yo'nat Ilem,* No. 22

DAY 229

The mind is the sky, the heart is the earth. We are taught to think with both, mind and heart, thereby bringing together the forces of Sky and Earth, unifying Above and Below, in which moment we become whole within ourselves.

—Eighteenth-century RABBI MORDECHAI YOSEF of Ischbitz
in *Mei Ha'Shi'lo'ach,* Vol. 1, beginning

DAY 230

Where your thought is, is precisely where *you* are—all of
yourself is there.

—Eighteenth-century Rabbi Yisro'el Ba'al Shem Tov,
quoted in *Mei Ha'Shi'lo'ach*, Vol. 1, beginning

DAY 231

Take pleasure in the joys of this world, but in the process do not forget the joys awaiting you in the next world. This is analogous to the father of a groom who prepares a huge banquet replete with wide varieties of delicacies. Prior to the wedding ceremony, the father walks about double-checking on all the preparations, even tasting of the delicacies readied for the feast to come. Do you suppose that while sampling the tasty foods of the wedding dinner that he for one moment forgets about the greater joy that is about to happen [the ceremony and the banquet]? Likewise, while you are savoring the pleasures of this lifetime, neglect not thoughts of the ultimate bliss yet to come.

—Eighteenth-century RABBI MORDECHAI YOSEF of Ischbitz in *Mei Ha'Shi'lo'ach,* Vol. 1, beginning

DAY 232

T'shuvah [Hebrew for what is called "repentance"] is more than remorse. It acknowledges that the possibility to have implemented wrongness, to begin with, had been granted by the Creator. As such, in turning your life around, you then realign your past action to where the Creator would have preferred it to be directed, in the first place. [This is the meaning of *t'shuvah*, which literally translates as "returning."]

—Eighteenth-century RABBI TZADOK HA'KOHAIN
in *Tzid'kat HaTzadik*, No. 100

DAY 233

If you draw fresh wisdom into the world, but your intent is public self-glorification, your wisdom is empty and void of Divine Influence. However, if you draw fresh wisdom into the world without any ulterior motive, then your wisdom—even if erroneous—is filled with Divine Influence and empowerment. For, as the sages taught, "The Compassionate One desires the heart" (Babylonian Talmud, *Chaggigah* 15b).

—Eighteenth-century RABBI TZADOK HA'KOHAIN
in *Tzid'kat HaTzadik*, No. 115

DAY 234

Caution: The more spiritually evolved you are than others, the more your susceptibility to impulses can cause your fallback (Babylonian Talmud, *Sukah* 52a). So don't be so sure of yourself until it's all over (Babylonian Talmud, *Avot* 2:1).

DAY 235

All creation is imbued with consciousness. Therefore, even a stone or a tree that caused injury to another creature will have to answer for its action.

—*Midrash Tana D'bei Eliyahu Rabbah*, Ch. 24

DAY 236

Every day, God calls to you, as it is written: "I called you and you turned away" (Proverbs 1:24). It is also written: "I called you and you did not answer" (Isaiah 65:12), and: "I called and no one responded" (Isaiah 66:4). How, then, do you know that God is calling you? When you are suddenly smitten with a wave of fresh inspiration from out of nowhere, know that God is calling you. You might want to respond with *hee'ney'nee,* "I am here" and open your heart to the love that waits to enter it, to the newness of the next moment as if it were your very first—and behold the magic that will then unfold for you!

—Eighteenth-century Rabbi Tzadok Ha'Kohain
in *Tzid'kat HaTzadik,* No. 222

DAY 237

Be careful what you ask for. It might be much more than you can handle. It is told that Caesar once asked Rabbi Yehoshua ben Chananyah: "You people claim that your god is like a lion. If so, what is so great about that? After all, one of my horsemen can easily slay a lion!" Rabbi Yehoshua replied: "Our god is likened not to just any ordinary lion but to the tiger, who we consider the lion of the Heavenly Forest." Caesar said: "I wish to see one. Show it to me." Rabbi Yehoshua said: "It is so fierce that you will not be able to so much as look at it." Caesar said: "I insist, nevertheless!" Rabbi Yehoshua prayed to the Creator to bring one forth, and instantly the tiger was conjured from its place in the spirit realm. When it approached within four hundred miles of the earth, it roared once and all the pregnant women of Rome miscarried, and all the walls of Rome collapsed. When the tiger approached within three hundred miles of the earth, the teeth of all the men of Rome fell out, and Caesar himself fell from off his throne. "I beg of you," cried Caesar, "please ask your god to restore this creature to its place." Rabbi Yehoshua prayed to the Creator and the tiger returned to the Heavenly Forest.

—Babylonian Talmud, *Chullin* 59b

DAY 238

Rabbi Uri of Strelisk (eighteenth century) was traveling by coach with several of his disciples when suddenly the horses came to an abrupt halt, and the driver spotted a bear coming toward them. Rabbi Uri stepped down from the wagon and walked straight toward the bear and stared into her eyes. The bear stopped, stared back for a while, and then walked off into the woods. When the disciples proclaimed the incident a miracle, Rabbi Uri said to them: "It is no miracle. Rather, anyone who walks the walk of balance between the extremes has no cause to be afraid of the bear. For the bear walks the walk of balance between the extremes: between abundance and scarcity, and between gluttony and abstention."

DAY 239

Rabbi Yehudah ben Tey'ma said: "When performing a sacred act, in service of the Creator, be bold like panther, and light as eagle, quick on the run like deer, and powerful like lion."

—Babylonian Talmud, *Avot* 5:23

DAY 240

Animals have their attributes, but don't forget that everything is relative and nothing is absolute. Once, Rabbi Illish (second century) was fleeing the Roman authorities when he came upon a raven. "Illish! Illish!" cried the raven, "The direction in which you are running is dangerous!" He ignored it, for he knew that the raven is the Contrary and one therefore does the opposite of what the raven says. Soon he came upon a dove who informed him that on this particular occasion, the raven was right. Rabbi Illish turned back and was spared.

—Babylonian Talmud, *Gittin* 54a

DAY 241

Trees and stones have feelings too. Be careful what you say about them. Rabbi El'azar ben Par'ta (third century) taught: "It is written 'and the men died, who had brought ill tidings concerning the land' (Numbers 14:37)—[they died] because they had slandered the trees and the stones."

—Babylonian Talmud, *Er'chin* 2:6

DAY 242

The school of Rabbi Yannai (second century) taught: "The phoenix lives a thousand years at a time. At the end of every thousand years, a great fire bursts forth from its nest and consumes it, leaving only a clump of ashes the volume of the bulk of an egg. And from this clump it grows new limbs and comes to life again."

—Midrash B'reishis Rabbah 19:5

DAY 243

Rabbi Yehudah (second century) taught: "If you see a pelican, it is a sign of compassion, that compassion has come into the world." Rabbi Abbahu taught: "If you see an eagle hovering around you, it is a sign of compassion." What is the difference? Storks have compassion only for their own, whereas the compassion of the eagle extends to all.

—Babylonian Talmud, *Chullin* 63a
and *Sefer Ha'Zohar,* Vol. 4, folio 233a; *Midrash Sif'ra,* No. 14

DAY 244

While it is alive, a sheep has one voice. After its life is over, it gains seven voices: the two horns become ritual sounding horns [*shofarot*]; the two leg bones become flutes; its hide becomes drums; its entrails become strings for musical instruments; and its intestines become strings for the harp.

—Babylonian Talmud, *Kinim* 3:6

DAY 245

The tiger is the lion of the Heavenly Forest. The unicorn is the stag of the Heavenly Forest.

—Babylonian Talmud, *Chullin* 59b

DAY 246

Here, then, is the mystery of why some people are buried in this land, and some in yet another land. For it is known that the First Human was formed out of earth gathered from the Four Winds of the world. It is also known that all human souls are sparks of the primeval soul of the First Human, and likewise our bodies are offshoots of the sparks of the primeval body of the First Human. Therefore, all human souls correspond to one part of the primordial human body or another, this one from the head, this one from the eye, and so on (*Midrash Tanchuma, Ki'Tissa*, No. 12, and *P'kudei*, No. 3). Thus, some people are made of the primordial thumb and, in turn, of the particular earth from a particular region of the world from which it was formed. Others are from the primordial ear and its particular earth and the specific region of the Four Winds of the world from which it was formed, and so on. Thus some people end up being buried here, some there, some elsewhere, each returning to the earth from which they originated in the primordial sense.

—*Kit'vei Ha'Ari, Sha'ar Ma'amarei Cha'zal, Sukkah* 53a

DAY 247

No matter where a person dies, the earth in that place cannot claim "This one is not made of my soil," for the human was created from earth gathered from all Four Winds of the world. Therefore, wherever a person dies, the earth of that very place finds the body familiar and receives it. As is written: "For you were taken out of the earth; you are earth, and to the earth shall you return" (Genesis 3:19).

—*Midrash Tanchuma, P'kudei,* No. 3 [end]

DAY 248

What is the ritual of the barley offering? One waves the barley shoots in its season, first inward and outward to ward off harsh winds harmful to the crops, then upward and downward to ward off harsh rains harmful to the crops. Others say: first inward and outward to the One to whom belongs all of the universe, then upward and downward to the One to whom belongs both the Upper Realms and the Lower Realms.

—*Midrash P'sik'ta D'Rav Kahana, Pis'ka Chet, Ha'Omer*, para. 11

DAY 249

What we do to the land we deem "personal property"
affects the rest of the planet, which knows no geographical
boundaries. What we do to our "private" land, in other
words, is not exempt from any ecological consequences
we might thereby wreak upon the rest of the planet. It is
analogous to a ship full of people sailing on the high seas
when one of the passengers began to drill a hole on the floor
of his section of the boat. His fellow passengers admonished
him: "Cosmic fool! What are you doing!?" He replied: "What
business is it of yours what I am doing? This is my section! I
paid for this space on the boat!" They said: "Of course it is
our business when what you are doing in your personal space
is going to destroy us all!"

—Second-century RABBI SHIM'ON BAR YO'CHAI
in *Midrash Vayik'ra Rabbah* 4:6

DAY 250

Everywhere is the center of the universe; every space is filled with the Divine Presence. There is no place on the earth that is void of the *Shecheenah* [the feminine quality of God].

—*Midrash P'sik'ta D'Rav Kahana, Pis'ka Alef,* Para. 4

DAY 251

Make no assumptions. Not even about someone you are in love with and who is as deeply in love with you. As the second-century Rabbi Channina taught: "A groom may not approach the wedding ceremonial space without first being invited to do so by the bride."

—*Midrash P'sik'ta D'Rav Kahana, Pis'ka Alef,* Para. 1

DAY 252

They asked Wisdom: "What is the consequence for those who err?" Wisdom replied: "Those who err shall be pursued by negativity" (Proverbs 13:21). They asked Prophecy: "What is the consequence for those who err?" Prophecy replied: "The soul that errs, is headed toward death" (Ezekiel 18:4). They asked Torah: "What is the consequence for those who err?" Torah replied: "Let the erring bring an offering and be put right" (Leviticus 1:4). They asked God: "What is the consequence for those who err?" God replied: "Let them turn back and be forgiven," as is written—"God redirects the wayward onto the right path" (Psalms 28:8).

—*Midrash P'sik'ta D'Rav Kahana, Shu'vah,* Para. 8

DAY 253

When Rabbi Channina took ill, Rabbi Yochanan went to see him and assured him that the more he suffered in this world the more his reward would be in the next world. Rabbi Channina replied: "I don't need this, and I don't need its reward." Rabbi Yochanan then said to him: "Give me your hand." He gave him his hand and Rabbi Yochanan lifted him out of his bed and he was healed (Babylonian Talmud, *B'rachot* 5a). The acronym for the words "he gave him his hand" is one of the seventy-two sacred mystery names of the Divine. It was the name Moses employed to conjure up the coffin in which the ancestor Joseph was buried, so that he might take the remains back with him to Canaan. This is a powerful incantation for healing someone: *y'hav lei ya'dei.* First one says to the bedridden one: "*Hav lee yad'cha* [bring to me your hand]" and when the sick one has extended the hand, take it into yours and say "*y'hav lei ya'dei v'uk'mei* ['he brought to him his hand and he raised him'])," during which you also concentrate on the Divine Name *YLY* [*yeh lee yo*].

—*Kit'vei Ha'Ari, Sha'ar Ma'amarei Cha'zal, B'rachot* 5b

DAY 254

Rabbi Yo'sei (second century) taught: "The Sacred Wellspring [God] has a tree. And this tree is bordered by the Four Winds of the world. And on this tree hang twelve clusters of pistachio nuts. And in each cluster are spirit beings of all grades who influence the worlds below in varying degrees. The clusters comprise nine nuts growing toward Place of Illumination [East], nine toward Place of Concealment [North], nine toward Place of Rising [South], and nine toward Place of Blending [West]—totaling thirty-six. And from them sprout forth all souls, for they grow upon this tree, as is written: 'I am like a blossoming cypress tree; your fruit issues forth from Me' (Hosea 14:9). From this we learn that all souls are the fruit of the Sacred Wellspring."

—Mid're'shei HaG'nizot, Ba'tei Midrashot,
Likuttei Midrashim Kit'vei Yad, B'reisheet, No. 2

DAY 255

When you combine the first letter of the Torah *V* with the last letter of the Torah *L* you get the word *vl* [*val*]—Empty. When you combine the last letter of the Torah *L* with the first letter of the Torah *V*, you get the word *lv* [*lev*]—Heart. Thus says the Sacred Wellspring: "My children, if you live by these two attributes, living with openness and acting with heart, then I will consider you to have fulfilled My deepest desire, as expressed in the Torah, and that you have done so in its entirety, from beginning to end."

—*Mid're'shei HaG'nizot, Ba'tei Midrashot, O'ti'ot D'Rebbe Akiva Ha'Shaleym, Nusach Alef,* on the letter *Bet* [end]

DAY 256

The Creator said: "If not for the songs and chants that you sing every day, I would not have created My world." Indeed, all of creation sings at all times, as is written: "From the ends of the earth we heard singing and chanting" (Isaiah 40:16).

—*Mid're'shei HaG'nizot, Ba'tei Midrashot, O'ti'ot D'Rebbe Akiva Ha'Shaleym, Nusach Alef,* on the letter *Alef* [beginning]

DAY 257

The Sacred Wellspring [God] is surrounded by spirits engulfed in great fires. And when a mortal dares to conjure them, they fan into even greater flames and react fiercely and descend from heavenly realm to heavenly realm with the intent of destroying the world with fire. And when they arrive on the earth and notice how the wings of the heavens are bound up with the wings of the earth, and the wings of the earth with the wings of the heavens—sealed with the seal of the Four Winds in the name *Eh'yeh Asher Eh'yeh* [I Will Be What I Will Be]—they instantly withdraw their wrath and conduct themselves with compassion toward the entire world, and especially toward the person who had aroused their fury by calling on them in the first place.

—Mid're'shei HaG'nizot, Ba'tei Midrashot, O'ti'ot D'Rebbe Akiva Ha'Shaleym, Nusach Alef, on the letter *Hey*

DAY 258

If the entire world was populated with fools, we would not recognize foolishness. If the entire world was populated with wise people, we would not recognize wisdom. Every opposite lends definition to the other, as is written: "This, too, opposite the other did God create" (Ecclesiastes 7:14).

—*Mid're'shei HaG'nizot, Ba'tei Midrashot, Midrash T'murah Ha'Shaleym,* Ch. 3

DAY 259

When the Creator wanted to bring the Great Flood, the Creator took two stars from the constellation of the Seven Sisters [Pleiades] and poured their waters onto the world. When the Creator wanted to stop the flood, the Creator took two stars from Bear [Big Dipper] and caused the floodwaters to recede.

—Babylonian Talmud, *B'rachot* 59b

DAY 260

During my first encounter with the Ba'al Shem Tov
(early eighteenth century), he asked me if I had studied the
Kabbalah. I said, "Yes, I had." There happened to be a book
on the table in front of him. He handed it to me and asked
me to read from it aloud. I did as he asked, and read a page
and a half to him when he interrupted me and said: "Not
right. Let me read it for you." He took the book from my
hands and began to read. In the middle of reading, he rose
and started to encircle me. Then he pressed on my shoulder
gently and lay me down on the bed and moved my body into
the shape of a circle. I was no longer able to see him; I began
to hear voices none of which was his, and I saw terrifying
flashes of light and flaming torches as he continued walking
around me, spinning me into realms I'd never visited before.

—Eighteenth-century Rabbi Dov Baer of Mezeritch
in *Shiv'chei Ha'Besh't*

DAY 261

At the birth of a girl, a cypress tree or other evergreen is planted, and at the birth of a boy, a cedar tree is planted. When they are ready to marry, two branches are cut from each tree to make up the four poles that hold up the wedding canopy.

—Babylonian Talmud, *Gittin* 57a

DAY 262

It is written: "Oil and incense gladden the heart" (Proverbs 27:9). God said: "Of all the offerings that you bring to me, none of them is as dear to me as the incense offering; for while all the offerings are for expiation of wrongdoings, or for thanksgiving, or for accompaniment of restitution, the incense offering is for joy alone."

—*Midrash Tanchuma, Tetzaveh,* No. 15

DAY 263

To draw in the *Shecheenah*, the feminine quality of the
Divine Presence, an incense offering is required. For
the Divine Presence does not completely manifest herself
within the realm of mortals without the aroma of incense.

—*Midrash Tanchuma, Tetzaveh*, No. 15

DAY 264

Prior to making an incense offering, it is important to chant, for the power of song draws forth the soul of the plants and herbs. And remember that the incense offering is the most potent antidote against evil forces.

—*Sefer Ha'Zohar*, Vol. 2, folio 219
and *Sefer Ha'Zohar Chadash, Shir HaShirim*, No. 67

DAY 265

With the arrival of the season of the blossoming [summer] it is customary to spread pleasant-smelling grasses and flowers across the floor of the prayer space.

—Fifteenth-century Rabbi Ya'akov HaLey'vee
in *Sefer Maharil, Minhagim, Hil'chot Shavu'ot,* No. 2

DAY 266

It is the custom to bring wood pieces and grasses to the meal space and to smoke them upon smoldering stones. When their smoke begins to rise, recite: "Source of Blessing are You, Infinite One, Source of our Powers, Council of the Universe, who creates aromatic grasses, aromatic trees, and aromatic wood."

—Fourteenth-century RABBI YA'AKOV BEN ASHER
in *Ar'ba Turim, Orach Chayyim,* No. 174

DAY 267

The deepest truths of the Kabbalah can only be communicated orally. All the teachings of the great Kabbalists are truths from one point of view and not truths from another point of view. They are truths as understood by the masters who taught them, but they are not truths in the way the student understands them. This is because only the ordinary surface layer of the Kabbalah, which does not represent the entirety of its true meaning, can be conveyed through texts. Whereas the underlying esoteric layers of the Kabbalah, which alone constitute its truths, cannot be communicated through the written word.

—Eighteenth-century Rabbi Ya'akov of Emden
in *Mit'pachat S'farim,* folios 77-78

DAY 268

In the time to come, there will be no more dying. And there will be no more sighing, wailing, or anguish, only singing and rejoicing. And there will be no more grief; no more weeping, and no more crying out of sadness or distress.

—Eighth-century B.C.E. YESHAYAHU HA'NA'VEE
in Isaiah 25:8, 35:10, and 65:19

DAY 269

All speculated times for the coming of the Messiah have already passed. There is nothing left for us to do but to engage in bettering ourselves and in deeds of loving kindness.

—Second-century Rabbi Abba Arey'kha
in Babylonian Talmud, *Sanhedrin* 97b

DAY 270

Three days before the coming of the Messiah, Elijah the prophet will issue three announcements from atop the mountains that shall be heard across the world. On the first day, he shall proclaim: "Peace has come to the world!" On the second day he shall proclaim: "Goodness has come to the world!" And on the third day, he shall proclaim: "Redemption has come to the world!"

—Midrash P'sik'ta Rabatee, Pis'kot 35-37

DAY 271

In the time to come, the Creator will gather all the birds and animals, all the creeping-crawlies, and all the peoples, and establish a new Covenant with them all.

—Seventh-century B.C.E. HO'SHEY'A HA'NA'VEE
in Hosea 2:20

DAY 272

Rabbi Yo'chanan ben Zakkai (first century) taught: "If you happen to be in the middle of planting new seeds and they announce to you that the Messiah has come, first complete your planting, then go and greet the Messiah." For there is nothing more precious than your personal process unfolding by your own efforts. More precious is this process here and now than eternal life in the World to Come.

—Babylonian Talmud,
Avot D'Rebbe Natan, Nus'cha Bet, 31:2 and *Avot* 4:22

DAY 273

In the end of days, the Creator will celebrate with all the creations. It shall be a rejoicing of a sort that has never before been experienced by any since the moment the creation of the universe first commenced.

—Third-century Rabbi Abba
in *Midrash Tanchuma, Va'Yera*, Ch. 38

DAY 274

In the end of days, the sun shall glow with healing energies
(Malachi 3:20); and living waters shall flow forth from
Jerusalem and split into rivers that will stream across the
planet bringing healing to all creatures who are ill (Ezekiel
47:9); and the leaves and fruits of trees shall be blessed with
direct, immediate healing powers (Ezekiel 47:12); and all
cities that have been destroyed—including Sodom and
Gomorah—shall be rebuilt, and their former inhabitants
restored to life (Ezekiel 16:55); and both predator and prey
shall live peacefully and unthreatened together, and share
their meals with one another (Isaiah 11:7).

—*Midrash Sh'mot Rabbah* 16:2

DAY 275

If you seek straight answers to the meaning of life, you're
not ready to know it. In the second century they asked Rabbi
Akiva: "Is everything preordained, or do we have free will?"
He replied: "Everything is preordained, and the choice
is yours."

—Babylonian Talmud, *Avot* 3:10

DAY 276

All the souls of the universe are the fruit of the Sacred
Wellspring. They are all as one, bound together in a shared
mystery, no one soul distinguishable from another, and neither
female nor male—all one. It is only when they are sent into our
universe that they become individuated from this oneness of
being and take on the qualities of the masculine and the
feminine. They then become male and female, combined
in a single soul.

—*Sefer Ha'Zohar,* Vol. 1, folio 85b

DAY 277

At the moment that the yearnings of lovers are roused, the longing of Below rises to merge with the longing of Above, and two souls manifest, one from Below, one from Above. And each soul is locked in embrace with the other to become as one Will that is inseparable. And then the feminine quality of the lovers gathers both, the soul formed from Above and the soul formed from Below, and becomes pregnant with them through the act of lovemaking. And the yearnings of both partners for one another merge as one, the longing of each locked in the embrace of the other.

—*Sefer Ha'Zohar,* Vol. 1, folio 85b

DAY 278

The soul born of the yearning between lovers is willed
into being by the Sacred Wellspring, and given form and
definition by mortal lovemaking. And then it is sent into
the world with the qualities of spirit and matter, of Sky and
Earth, combined with the qualities of the masculine and the
feminine. And as it manifests in the physical universe, it splits
into two separate souls, one with the predominant qualities
of the feminine, and one with the predominant qualities of
the masculine, each imbued with the attributes of the other,
like a single flame split in two by separate wicks. And once
on earth, they seek out one another, to join as soul mates,
to become again as one.

—*Sefer Ha'Zohar,* Vol. 1, folio 85b

DAY 279

It is important during lovemaking to intend one's yearnings from a place of truth, from a place of love, with the intention of gifting form to new souls, form imbued with harmony of spirit and body, and locked in eternal embrace with the Sacred Wellspring of all that was, is, and will be.

—*Sefer Ha'Zohar,* Vol. 1, folio 85b

DAY 280

There is a stone that has existed from the days of the first ancestors, and it is called *Ehven Sheh'tee'yah,* Stone of Nurturance. And it is three fingers larger in circumference than the earth. Why is it called the Stone of Nurturance? For out of this stone did our universe nurture itself into fruition. Come and see: this stone has seven eyes.

—Babylonian Talmud, *Tosef'ta Yoma* 2:12;
Sefer Ha'Zohar, Vol. 1, folio 231a

DAY 281

When the prophet Jonah was trapped in the belly of the great fish, she swam beneath the area of the earth upon which the Stone of Nurturance was embedded. This is the rock from which all of Creation had been fashioned; this is the rock upon which sit the seven mountains; it is the center of all centers. And Jonah peered out of the belly of the great fish and beheld the Stone of Nurturance suspended above the Abyss, and he saw the spirits of the ancestors praying over the great stone. And the Infinite One spoke to Jonah, and said: "Pray here, and you will be answered."

—*Midrash Tanchuma, Va'yik'ra*, Ch. 8

DAY 282

Rabbi Pinchas of Koretz heard that one of his disciples had secluded himself in a cave for days without food or water. He hurried to the cave and admonished the emaciated young man: "This is not our way! We don't starve ourselves to become holy!" The disciple replied: "But you yourself would tell us many stories about your own teacher, Rabbi Yisro'el Ba'al Shem Tov, how he would go for weeks without eating or drinking and how he became such a great miracle worker!" Rabbi Pinchos said: "My dear son, my teacher would indeed spend days in the mountains without eating or drinking, the only difference is that he would always take food along with him but would forget to eat!"

—Oral tradition

DAY 283

We have so much trouble with one God; can you imagine
with two gods?

—Rabbi Shlomo Carlebach; oral tradition

DAY 284

All beings in nature perform the will of God, as is written:
"All the works of the Infinite One act for the sake of the
Creator" (Proverbs 16:4), and as is recounted in the Talmud
about the scorpion that was crossing the river, who said:
"I am on my way to perform the will of my Creator"
(Babylonian Talmud, *Chullin* 7a), for such is its nature. We
also find this concept in the Book of the Zohar (Vol. 3, folio
222b), and in the story of the frog who informs King David
that she sings far more praises to the Creator than he, singing
to God all day and all night (*Midrash Tehilim,* Ch. 148)—
meaning literally that even her croaking sounds are for the
sake of the Creator. Likewise, everything we humans do that
we deem "natural," that we are inclined to do because of our
nature, such as eating, drinking, and sex, is considered a
sacred act, as an act of performing the will of the Creator.

—Eighteenth-century RABBI TZADOK HAKOHAIN
in *Tsid'kat HaTzadik,* No. 173

DAY 285

It is so awesome to be created by God that you forget you're created.

—Rabbi Shlomo Carlebach; oral tradition

DAY 286

We are here for the purpose of not knowing why. In not knowing why, all of our actions and our choices become our very own, untainted by ulterior motives of doing something because of the promise of heavenly reward, or not doing something because of some threat of heavenly punishment.

—second-century B.C.E. ANTIG'NOS of Sukko
in Babylonian Talmud, *Avot* 1:3

DAY 287

Tradition is a marker we leave behind us in our previous lives so that when we come back we have some notion of where we left off. We need to look at tradition, therefore, not as a relic of the past but as a catalyst for the future.

—Rabbi Zalman Schachter-Shalomi; oral tradition

DAY 288

If you make a mistake the first time, do not be concerned about it. Rather, be concerned about it if you repeat it a second time. If you do something right the first time, do not pride yourself about it. Rather, be proud of yourself if you repeat it a second time.

—Second-century Ben Zoma
in Babylonian Talmud, *Avot D'Rebbe Natan, Nus'cha Bet,* 33:3

DAY 289

God created universes and destroyed them, created universes and destroyed them, until this universe came into being.

—Third-century Rabbi Avahu in *Midrash Kohelet Rabatti* 3:14

DAY 290

Rabbi Avahu (third century) said: "Greater is rainfall than
the resurrection of the dead, for the resurrection of the dead
happens only to the righteous whereas rainfall happens for
both the righteous as well as for the wicked."

—Babylonian Talmud, *Ta'anit* 7a

DAY 291

One day Rabbi Chiyya (first century) was sitting at the passageway leading to the gate of Usha. He noticed Rabbi El'azar walking by and that a bird was hovering over his head as he walked. Rabbi Chiyya remarked to him: "It appears that even when you are walking on the road, everyone yearns to follow in your footsteps, including the animals." Rabbi El'azar turned his head to see the bird and replied: "Certainly this bird has come as a messenger from God, for God communicates through all varieties of messengers."

—*Sefer Ha'Zohar,* Vol. 2, folios 25a

DAY 292

In the eyes of God, personal insight is more precious than Divine Revelation. For if you depend exclusively upon the scriptures and the teachings of religions and of the masters but have no personal insights of your own, it is all worthless.

—Second-century RABBI AKIVA
in *Midrash O'ti'ot D'Rebbe Akiva, O't Bet*

DAY 293

See how marvelous is a good woman. For it is in her that the Divine Will is exemplified.

—Fourth-century RAVA in Babylonian Talmud, *Yevamot* 63b

DAY 294

The Hebrew Creation story tells us of a river that emerges from out of the deepest of mysteries, from the Infinite Being of all beings. This beautiful wellspring carries us through our earthly existence and remains pure always, undisturbed by the turmoil of our life journey, gifting us with a core sense of balance and reminding us of God's unconditional love. In down-to-earth terms, this is your heart of hearts, which is always pure, always virtuous, even through the mistakes we sometimes make. To this heart of hearts we can always turn and return again, and from within her we can remember and rediscover the precious primordial "I" with which God gifted us at our creation. As is written: "A pure heart did God create in me; a spirit of authenticity did God renew deep in me" (Psalms 51:12).

DAY 295

Ah'nee Wa'ho Hoshee'a' Na is a powerful chant that was
originally sung by the ancient Hebrews in the season of
autumn during the seven-day harvest festival of *Sukkot.*
During this ceremony they would gather willows, lean them
against the altar, and then dance in a circle around the altar.
The words literally mean: "I and the All (God), please help us
now!" The chant is actually an important teaching reminder,
that since God participates in our sorrows, in time of need,
we therefore call out to both participants in the situation, our
Self and God (Jerusalem Talmud, *Sukkah* 4:3). This is based
on the teaching in the Torah that one cannot be helped
without also *wanting* to be helped, as is written: "When you
see your fellow struggling with their load, help *along* with
them" (Exodus 23:5 and Deuteronomy 22:4). When you seek
God's help, too, you must help yourself *along* with God's
intervention. By chanting *Ah'nee Wa'ho,* you are in essence
calling upon that attribute of God that joins with you in the
experience of your struggle. You are in essence calling God by
the name that describes God as immanent, as partners with
you in the moment of your need. You are calling to the God
who echoes back to you a sense of *Ah'nee Wa'ho,* a sense of
"me and you."

DAY 296

There are eighteen thousand worlds that the Creator made and continues to guide constantly (Babylonian Talmud, *Avodah Zarah* 3b). All of these worlds are filled with the glory of the Creator no less than our own world. It also seems clear that these eighteen thousand worlds are not part of our known universe but that each of them is rather a complete universe with its own "earth" and stars and planets, unrelated to our own universe.

—Twelfth-century RABBI YEHUDAH BARZELAI
on *Sefer Yetzirah,* folios 171-173; Halberstamm edition

DAY 297

After Adam and Eve ate of the forbidden fruit and were expelled from the Garden of Eden, two angels, Aza and Aza'el, approached God and said: "See how the human is incapable of living in balance upon your earth. Were you to send us to live upon your earth, we would make you proud, for we are higher beings than they and would not transgress your will under any circumstances." God accepted their challenge and "dropped" them from the heavens so that they "fell" to the earth, and thus they were called the *nefilim,* or "fallen ones" (Genesis 6:4). But the force of physical impulses quickly overtook the two angels and they failed abysmally. Rabbi El'azar (second century) said: "I have heard a great mystery teaching from my master Rabbi Shim'on, that these two angels were never again able to return to the spirit world, and that they continue to walk the earth to this day. What do they do? They impart the wisdom of sorcery to those who yearn to know it."

—*Sefer Ha'Zohar,* Vol. 1, folio 58a

DAY 298

The primary source of confusion in our search for the meaning of the universe as a whole, or even of its parts, is rooted in our mistaken assumption that all of existence is for our sake alone. For if we examine our universe objectively, we will discover how very small a part of it we really are. The truth is, that all of humankind and all the species of life-forms on earth are as naught in comparison with all of the continuing cosmic existence.

—Twelfth-century RABBI MOSHE IBN MAIMON
in *Moreh N'vuchim* 3:12

DAY 299

The essence of God permeates every realm, every strata of the spirit realm, within the angels and between them, within the celestial spheres and between them. It penetrates all the elements of the physical universe, and within the earth herself as well as between the earth and her children, down through the ultimate void of the Abyss.

—Sixteenth-century Rabbi Moshe Cordovero
in *Pardes Rimonim* 6:8

DAY 300

The Tree of Life and the Tree of Knowledge of Good and Evil are actually one and the same tree. Eating of the "forbidden fruit" implies severing something from its primordial unity, and in the story of the Garden of Eden it implies therefore the act of separating the two attributes of the one tree, the attribute of Life—oneness—and the attribute of Knowledge—individuation. According to the story, the dangers inherent in the fruit of the Tree of Knowledge appear unrelated to the act of encountering her fruit, but are rather related to the act of ingesting her fruit. As long as both realms are one, there is no danger of losing oneself to the evils of particularism and its dormant sense of superiority over the Other. Once severed from one another, and divided into two separate trees, the relationship with the Other is in danger of becoming hydraulic. This is the mystery of the Tree of Life and the Tree of Knowledge of Good and Evil.

—Thirteenth-century Rabbi Ez'ra ben Shlomo of Gerona
in *Sod Etz Ha'Da'at*

DAY 301

Rava created a humanlike creature from earth and animated it through Kabbalistic sorcery. It appeared before Rabbi Zey'ra and stood there, bedazzled. The rabbi spoke to it but it did not respond. Rabbi Zey'ra said: "Certainly you must be a creation of one of my colleagues. Return to the earth." It crumbled to dust.

—Babylonian Talmud, *Sanhedrin* 65b

DAY 302

A chicken farmer once approached Rabbi Yitzchak Luria
(sixteenth century) and asked to be admitted into his mystery
school. The rabbi gazed into the windows of his soul and said:
"I see that you are a good candidate, except for one minor
flaw which you must first rectify." The farmer spent the next
several days trying desperately to figure out what the flaw
might be. Finally, he returned to the sage and asked for a
clue. Rabbi Yitzchak asked him what he did for a living. "I
raise chickens," the farmer replied. "And what," asked the
rabbi, "is the very first thing that you do in the morning upon
awakening?" The farmer said: "I taste neither food nor drink
but go directly to the synagogue to worship God." The rabbi
said: "Therein lies your flaw. Because the very first thing that
you should be doing in the morning is not praying to God
but feeding your chickens."

—*Shiv'chei Ha'Ari*

DAY 303

Rabbi Shim'on bar Yo'chai and his son Rabbi El'azar (second century) were hiding from the Roman authorities. They were buried up to their necks in a cave where they were brought food and water by their wives. During their years in hiding they could do little more than meditate day and night. At the end of twelve years they were informed that a new Caesar was elected in Rome and that the decree against the rabbis of Israel had been rescinded. When they emerged from the cave, they had become so spiritual that they felt nothing but indignation toward anything material and everything they gazed at burst into flames, destroying entire fields and sending farmers scurrying to safety. "Woe onto those who barter the eternal life in the Infinite Realm for mundane toil in the Temporary Realm," they exclaimed. Suddenly, a heavenly voice was heard, proclaiming: "Have you emerged from hiding to destroy my world?! Return to the cave!" They returned to the cave and spent the next year grounding themselves, so that when they emerged a second time, whomever they gazed at became healed.

—Babylonian Talmud, *Shabbat* 33b–34a

DAY 304

This is the secret of the rooster's call: At the time when God comes to the Garden of Eden to visit those who have lived in balance, all the trees of the Garden of Eden bring forth their fragrance and break into song and praise. At that very moment, here on earth, the rooster is awakened by the heavenly chanting and joins in, singing its praise in seven calls.

—*Midrash Perek Shirah* 4:1

DAY 305

This is the prayer song of the dove: "Teacher of the Universe, better that my sustenance be bitter like olives but come from your hands, than be sweet like honey and come from the hands of mortals."

—*Midrash Perek Shirah,* Ch. 4; Babylonian Talmud, *Eruvin* 18b

DAY 306

This is the prayer song of the lizard: "Infinite Being, you are the Source of my Power; I exalt you; I acknowledge your essence, for you have performed wonders, and have proven the trustworthiness of the counsel of the ancients" (Isaiah 28:1).

—*Midrash Perek Shirah* 4:20

DAY 307

This is the prayer song of the deer: "And as for me, I shall chant about your strength, and sing until morning about your loving-kindness, because you have been for me like a high fortress, and a refuge in the day of my distress" (Psalms 59:17).

—Midrash Perek Shirah 5:11

DAY 308

This is the prayer song of the elephant: "How magnanimous are your works, O Infinite Being, your thoughts are very deep" (Psalms 92:6).

—*Midrash Perek Shirah* 5:12

DAY 309

This is the prayer song of the dog: "Come, everyone, let us bow down and humble ourselves; kneel before the Infinite Being, our Creator" (Psalms 95:6).

—*Midrash Perek Shirah* 6:8

DAY 310

This is the prayer song of the fox: "Woe onto those who build their homes absent of rightness, and with chambers absent of justice, and those who work their fellow creature without compensation, without payment to those hired" (Jeremiah 22:13).

—*Midrash Perek Shirah* 5:16

DAY 311

This is the prayer song of the snake: "Infinite Being supports all those who are fallen, and straightens those who are bent" (Psalms 145:14).

—*Midrash Perek Shirah* 6:2

DAY 312

Rabbi Abba Arey'kha (second century) was summoned to a region that was experiencing a drought. He instructed the people to fast, but no rain fell. Then a man stepped forward to lead the people in prayer, and recited: "God restores the wind!" And the wind began to blow. He then exclaimed: "God sends down the rain!" And the rain began to fall. Curious about the stranger's supernal powers, Abba Arey'kha asked him: "What is your work?" He replied: "I am a teacher of young children, and I teach the children of the poor in the same manner as I teach the children of the rich. And if anyone is unable to pay for their lessons, I will accept no form of payment from them."

—Babylonian Talmud, *Ta'anit* 23a

DAY 313

Greater are the deeds of the righteous than the Creation of Heaven and Earth (Babylonian Talmud, *Ketuvot* 5a). What did the sages mean by this? For the creation of Heaven and Earth was the act of creating something out of nothing, whereas the deeds of the righteous create nothing out of something. All the actions of the righteous, even seemingly ordinary actions such as eating, transform the corporeal—the Some-Thing—into the realm of the Divine—the No-Thing.

—Eighteenth-century RABBI DOV BAER of Mezeritch
in *Likuttei Amarim* 2b

DAY 314

The challenge of the human is to create in every organ, in every limb, a sacred space for God to fill. Before lifting one's hand against another, or to comfort another, one ought to take a moment to create such a space in the hand, inviting God to fill the limb and thereby the action that the limb or organ is about to perform. The hand raised to strike would then raise in your consciousness the question, would God want you to strike the other with the Divine Presence? The hand stretched forth to comfort someone would then be empowered yet further with the added quality of Divine Comfort. Therefore, invite God to be sovereign over—and to whom you would answer regarding—the actions of all of your organs and limbs so that no part of you is absent of the Divine Presence.

—*Tikunei Zohar,* folio 132a

DAY 315

When the vision-bringer and the shaman encounter the spirit realm, they begin to weaken in their body selves. They shift their form, both spiritual and physical, shape-shifting until they become completely garbed in the form that is channeled to them, ultimately taking on the very form of the spirit that comes to them. It is this spirit form that enables them to then translate the vision or prophetic influx from the spirit realm. This spirit also becomes deeply manifested in their hearts in a spiritual sense so that its image takes the form of a visual experience for them. When the communication of the spirit is complete, the shamans are restored shape by shape to their original form and all their bodily powers return to their original state. It is only thereafter that the vision-bringer can speak the visions to the people in normal human language.

—Thirteenth-century Rabbi Yitzchak HaKohain of Soria,
quoted in *Avo'dat HaKo'desh*
by sixteenth-century Rabbi Me'ir ibn Gabbai

DAY 316

Why was Moses considered the greatest of all prophets
and prophetesses among the Israelites (Deuteronomy 34:10)?
Because, when all of the other prophets of Israel would look
beyond the Veil, they would think that they caught a glimpse
of God. But Moses was so great a prophet that when he
would look beyond the Veil, he would know for certain that
he had not caught a glimpse of God.

—Eleventh-century Rabbi Shlomo Yitzchaki
commenting on Babylonian Talmud, *Yevamot* 49b

DAY 317

Every person has an image of their self in the spirit realm, and this spirit guides that person's star. And at times, when the spirit is sent into the physical realm, it will then manifest in the very form of the earthly person whose image it represents, and offer guidance to the earthly self.

—Thirteenth-century RABBI ELIEZER of Worms
in *Choch'mat HaNefesh,* folios 17d-18a;
sixteenth-century RABBI CHAYYIM VITAL
in his introduction to *Sha'ar K'dushah*

DAY 318

Two souls exist in the earth being, Wind Spirit and Breath Spirit. While a person dreams, Wind Spirit journeys from one end of the universe to the other, and Breath Spirit remains, dwelling deep within the chamber of chambers.

—Midrash Olam Katan, No. 4

DAY 319

If you seek to live a life of truth with purity and sincerity, you will be shown the River of Light. When it is shown to you, begin to walk along its banks, veering neither to the left nor to the right but following its every bend. Eventually, you will then be shown the sacred place of mystery from which the river flows, and be taken to its very source from where the waters originate.

—Thirteenth-century RABBI YOSEF GIKATILA
in *Sha'arei Orah,* folio 20b

DAY 320

It is written: "I am the Infinite One who makes All; who alone stretched forth the expanse of the heavens; who layered the length and breadth of the earth by myself" (Isaiah 44:24). This is what God said: "It was I alone who planted the tree of existence, so that the entire universe would derive pleasure from it. And I carved everything within this tree and called its name The All. Because the very existence of all is suspended from this tree; all come from it, all are in need of it, all gaze upon it with hope, and all souls are derived from it."

—First-century RABBI NECHUN'YA BEN HA'KANAH
in *Sefer Ha'Bahir, Mishnah 22*

DAY 321

Behold the Sacred Ancient One—the mystery of all mysteries, who is separate from everything and yet at the same time not separated from anything, for all is joined within God and God is joined within all. For God is everything, the Ancient of all Ancients and the most hidden of all that is hidden; who is without shape and yet with shape. God has shape in order to sustain the universe, and God has no shape because God is not subject to the Realm of Existence.

—*Sefer Ha'Zohar,* Vol. 3, folio 228a

DAY 322

Long before time and existence, when the Ancient of all Ancients chose to become manifest as Creator, the Creator formed nine blazing lights from Its own essence. And these primeval lights shine forth from the Creator and extend continuously to all directions, akin to a flame. Yet when one approaches the glowing lights of a flame to study them, one realizes there is actually nothing there but the flame itself. Likewise, the Holy Ancient One is a spiritual flame, concealed beyond all that is hidden, knowable solely through these lights that emanate from Its essence only to reveal themselves momentarily and then immediately conceal themselves again. And these lights are known as the Sacred Names of God, and this is how all is ultimately one.

—*Sefer Ha'Zohar,* Vol. 3, folio 228a

DAY 323

The secret of astrology is this: The universe emanates constantly from the No End who is always dynamic, never static. Thus, the universe is in constant motion and the arrangements of its planets and stars are constantly shifting. Therefore, when we are born, we are born into a whole new universe formed at that moment anew by the changes effected in the arrangements of the stars and planets that in turn have shifted in the hour of our birth because of the ever-dynamic dance of No End.

—Sixteenth-century Rabbi Chayyim Vital
in *Etz Ha'Chayyim* 1:1:5, folio 15a

DAY 324

One time, a deathly ill boy was brought to Rabbi Yisro'el Ba'al Shem Tov (eighteenth century) for healing. The rabbi instructed his disciples to prepare a flaming torch, and he then journeyed into the forest. Once deep inside the woods, Rabbi Yisro'el affixed the torch to a tree and performed a number of rituals and meditations [intended to reconnect the boy's soul to the primeval Tree from which all souls emanate, for the soul is like a flame of God (Proverbs 20:27)]. With the help of God, the ritual worked and the boy became healed and his life spared. Some years after Rabbi Yisro'el had passed on, a similar situation was brought before his foremost disciple Rabbi Dov Baer of Mezeritch. And he said: "I do not know how to perform the particular rituals and meditations of my master, but I will rely on the efficacy of affixing the torch to the tree," and his patient was healed. Following the passing of Rabbi Dov Baer, one of his successors, Rabbi Moshe Leib of Sassov, was confronted with a similar situation. And he said: "I have no strength in me to venture into the forest, altogether. But I will rely on the efficacy of simply telling the story," and his patient was also healed.

—Eighteenth-century Rabbi Yisro'el of Rizhin in *K'nesset Yisro'el*, folio 12a; bracketed interpolation based on the commentary of Professor Moshe Idel, Hebrew University, in *Kabbalah: New Perspectives*, p. 397, note 94

DAY 325

The first-century rabbi Hillel the Elder taught: "If I am not for myself, then who is? And if I am only for myself, then what am I? And if I don't do what needs to get done now, then when will I get to do it?"

—Babylonian Talmud, *Avot* 1:14

DAY 326

If you were to plant an apple seed, much to your dismay
what begins to grow at first is not an apple but some
brownish looking thing that even after a year in no way
remotely resembles an apple. The "thing" continues to grow
and grow and eventually branch out but offers no sign of ever
becoming the fruit from whose seed it sprouted. At this point,
you can either give up and walk away, or you can continue
nurturing the tree with faith that the apple will emerge some-
day. Even as the branches thin out and become twigs, seeming
to indicate that the tree is thinning out and closing up shop,
you will cling tenaciously to your faith. Then one day a leaf
appears, but still without any sign of an apple. Finally the apple
appears. Likewise is it with your hopes and dreams. You have
a vision, and often the process of nurturing that vision to
realization in no way resembles the hoped for vision itself. But
with patience and faith, know that the process is the tree that
will eventually drop an apple on your lap.

DAY 327

Once a man was shipwrecked on a distant island. When he regained consciousness, he found himself surrounded by the natives of the island who immediately removed his shredded garb and bedecked him in royal cloth. Then they brought him to a castle where he lived happily ever after, replete with wives, children, and immense wealth. Until one day, it began to concern him: What was the catch? He inquired of his servant who informed him that there had been others just like him. They were made king or queen of the island for a period of ten years, after which they were sent back to sea on a raft with nothing but the shreds of clothing with which they came. The king grew disturbed by this. He loved his wives and children deeply, and cherished his riches. What was he to do? The servant replied: "If I were you, I would send it all home while you were still king." The king instantly shipped his family and his belongings back to his homeland, and when his time was over he went gladly to the raft and gladly surrendered his royal garb, for he knew he would soon be living uninterruptedly with all that he loved. This parable is your life. Send home now to the eternal realm whatever it is you cherish here in the temporal realm, by acknowledging the Source of all your blessings every time you experience them.

—Fourteenth-century RABBI BACH'YA IBN YOSEF PAQUDA
in *Cho'vot Hal'vavot, Sha'ar A'vodat Elo'heem,* Ch. 9

DAY 328

Eliezer the servant of Abraham (seventeenth century, B.C.E.) once asked Shem, the son of Noah: "Why does the phoenix never die?" Shem replied: "During the Great Flood, we were busy day and night feeding the myriad species of animals on the Ark. One day, during his feeding rounds, my father Noah discovered the phoenix sleeping in a corner of the Ark when it occurred to him that he had never brought it any food. My father asked the phoenix why it had not requested any food all this time. The phoenix answered, 'I was aware of how busy you were and decided not to trouble you further.' My father then blessed the phoenix and said: 'Because you were so concerned about my burden, may it be the Creator's will that you never die.'" Thus it is written: "I will multiply the days of my life like those of the phoenix" (Job 29:18).

—*Midrash Yal'kot Shim'onee, No'ach*, No. 59

DAY 329

Why at the beginning did God create flocks of geese, herds of deer, schools of fish, prides of lions, and only a single human? So that no one can say to another "My ancestor is superior to yours."

—Babylonian Talmud, *Sanhedrin* 38a

DAY 330

Every human is obliged to declare: "Because of me alone would the entire universe have been worth creating." But why was the human created singular, to begin with? To remind you of how exalted you are, having been the crescendo of Creation! But if it goes to your head, remember that the mosquito preceded you.

—Babylonian Talmud, *Sanhedrin* 38a

DAY 331

Why in the beginning was the human created singular? To demonstrate the preciousness of the human, that destroying a single human being would be akin to destroying an entire world, and saving a single human would be akin to saving an entire world.

—Babylonian Talmud, *Sanhedrin* 38a

DAY 332

When the Creator was about to create the human, the Creator first formed a council of angels and consulted with them: "Do you think I should create the human?" They said: "What is so special about the human that you should even consider such a thing?" The Creator touched them and they vanished. Then the Creator formed a second council of angels and consulted with them: "Do you think I should create the human?" They said: "Why would you risk such an endeavor? They would only abuse your world and misuse the gift of living." The Creator touched them and they vanished. Then the Creator formed a third council of angels and consulted with them: "Do you think I should create the human?" They said: "Well, seeing what happened to the others . . . yes, do as you wish. Good idea." And so the Creator made the human and the human abused the world and misused the gift of living, and brought the Great Flood upon the whole earth. At that point, the third council of angels approached the Creator and said: "See how the opinion of the other angels was correct." The Creator said: "I love the human. Even until they are elder, I will remain with them, unchanged; even until they have reached a ripe old age, I will tolerate them; I have created them, I will carry them, and I will put up with them and be there for them always" (Isaiah 46:4).

—Babylonian Talmud, *Sanhedrin* 38b

DAY 333

When the first humans were evicted from Paradise, they
noticed the days were growing shorter, the nights longer, and
the darkness thicker. They exclaimed: "Woe to us. See what
we have done by eating of the forbidden fruit, for Creation
has begun to unravel, and gradually everything is returning to
chaos, darkness, and soon total void!" They sat and grieved
for eight days, presuming God was punishing the world for
what they'd done. Following the winter solstice, they noticed
the days growing longer, the nights shorter, and the darkness
gradually easing. They said: "How wondrous are the ways of
the world! We erred in our presumptions." And they
observed eight days of celebration and joy. The following
year, they observed both, the eight days prior to the winter
solstice and the eight days following the winter solstice as
days of festive celebration.

—Babylonian Talmud, *Avodah Zarah* 8a

DAY 334

Rabbi Shim'on bar Yo'chai (second century) said: "A precious stone hung from the neck of our ancestor Abraham. And anyone who was sick became healed by merely looking up at this stone. When Abraham passed on, the Creator took the stone and suspended it from the sun." Abbaye said: "Thus the proverb, 'As the sun rises, the sick person, too, rises.'"

—Babylonian Talmud, *Baba Bat'ra* 16b

DAY 335

In the school of Elijah it was taught: "I call as my witnesses
the heavens and the earth, that anyone—whether they be
Jewish or of some other people, man or woman, manservant
or maidservant—is capable of channeling upon their self
Divine Inspiration, for revelatory experiences are gifted to us
based not on our gender, or on our religious affiliation or
social status, but on our life choices and actions."

—*Midrash Tana D'bei Eliya'hu*, Ch. 9

DAY 336

Divine Revelation, or the Word of God, is no different than raw wheat or flax. From wheat one derives bread and cakes of wide varieties, and from flax one derives cloth of wide varieties. Likewise the God Word was intended for us to derive endless possibilities of interpretation and application.

—*Midrash Tana D'bei Eliya'hu Zuta*, Ch. 2

DAY 337

Once, a man came to Elee'sha the Man of God (ninth century, B.C.E.) and brought him a gift of twenty loaves of barley bread from the first harvest. Elee'sha turned to his disciple and said: "Give the bread to the people so they may eat of it." The apprentice looked puzzled and said: "How can I divide these twenty loaves among a hundred people?" Elee'sha replied: "Give the bread to the people so they may eat of it, because the Infinite One has said, 'They shall eat and also have some of it left over.'" And the disciple distributed the bread and there was enough for all.

—Hebrew Scriptures, 2 Kings 4:42–44

DAY 338

Once, a widow came to Elee'sha the Man of God (ninth century, B.C.E.) and cried to him: "My husband is dead and left us with a huge debt, and now the creditor has threatened to seize one of my sons as an indentured servant!" Elee'sha said: "What do you have in your house?" She said: "I own nothing but a flask of oil." He said: "Go and borrow from your neighbors as many empty pots as you can gather. Then seclude yourself in your house with all these vessels and fill them all full of oil from your flask." The woman did as she was instructed; they kept bringing her containers and she kept pouring from her flask. When the vessels were all full, she said to her son: "Bring me another container." He said: "There are no more vessels"—and the oil ceased to flow. She came to Elee'sha and told him. And he said: "Now go sell the oil and pay off your debt, and you and your children can live off the rest."

—Hebrew Scriptures, 2 Kings 4:1-7

DAY 339

Although very poor, Rabbi Hanina ben Do'sa was a worker of miracles. Once, his wife asked him if he could possibly work some miracle to get hold of some of the premium stored up for them in Heaven, so that they might be able to use it in advance during their time on earth. Rabbi Hanina prayed and a hand emerged from the sky grasping the leg of a golden table. He took the leg from the hand and put it aside to sell its gold on the morrow. That night, he had a vision of everyone in Heaven seated at sturdy golden tables while he and his wife were seated at a golden table with only three legs. When he came to, he shared the vision with his wife and asked: "Is it alright with you that everyone in Heaven has a table with all its legs while our table has a leg missing?" She said: "What should we do? Can you pray that the leg be taken back?" He prayed, and a hand appeared from the heavens and took it back. When the elders heard about this, they exclaimed: "Greater is the miracle of the leg being taken back than the leg being given in the first place, for we have a tradition that Heaven gives but never takes back."

—Babylonian Talmud, *Ta'anit* 25a

DAY 340

Three things were created before the Creation of the world: Water, Wind, and Fire. Water conceived and bore thick darkness; Fire conceived and bore light; Wind conceived and bore wisdom.

—*Midrash Sh'mot Rabbah* 15:22

DAY 341

Four regions of the earth were created. One facing the east, one facing the west, one facing the south, and one facing the north. From the region facing East, light goes forth into the world. From the region facing South, dews of blessing go forth into the world. From the region facing West, hail, rain, snow, cold, and heat go forth into the world. As for the region facing North, God chose to leave it incomplete, as if to say: "Anyone who claims to be God, let them come and finish this part of the world that I left unfinished."

—*Midrash Pirkei Rebbe D'Rebbe Eliezer,* Ch. 3

DAY 342

A dream is one-sixtieth prophecy. In fact, someone sleeping in Babylon might experience a dream that is taking place in Spain. When Rabbi Sh'mu'el (third century) would have a bad dream, he would wake up and say: "Dreams are false." When he would have a good dream, he would wake up and say: "I wonder if dreams are true?"

—Babylonian Talmud, *B'rachot* 57b, *Nidah* 30b, and *B'rachot* 55a

DAY 343

Rava (fourth century) went to Bar Hadaya the dream interpreter and said: "I dreamt I saw two turnip tops." Bar Hadaya said: "It means you will be clubbed twice." He went on his way and came upon two blind men scuffling. When Rava tried to separate them, they beat him with their staffs once, then twice, and raised their sticks for a third blow when Rava shouted: "Enough! I only dreamt of two!" Some time later, he was traveling with Bar Hadaya when the latter dropped a scroll. Rava picked it up and as he did so it unrolled to a passage that read: "The dream follows its interpretation." He then admonished Bar Hadaya: "Idiot! It was your interpretation that caused my grief!"

—Babylonian Talmud, *B'rachot* 56b

DAY 344

Rabbi Yannai (third century) came to an inn and ordered something to drink. The innkeeper began to cast a spell upon the rabbi as he lifted his cup to drink. Rabbi Yannai, noticing that her lips were moving as if to murmur some incantations, spilled some of the drink onto the floor and watched the spill turn into tiny scorpions. He said: "As I have drunk of yours, I dare you to drink of mine." She agreed and took a sip from his cup while he muttered some incantations. Suddenly the woman dropped the cup and turned into a donkey. Rabbi Yannai rode on her through the streets until her friend recognized her and undid the spell. Lo and behold! Now Rabbi Yannai was seen by all riding on the shoulders of a woman, much to his embarrassment!

—Babylonian Talmud, *Sanhedrin* 67b

DAY 345

Rabbi Yitzchak (fourth century) taught: "If you want to become wise, turn toward the south when you pray; if you want to become rich, turn toward the north when you pray." Rabbi Yehoshua ben Ley'vee said: "One should then always turn toward the south since it is through wisdom that one stands a much better chance of acquiring wealth."

—Babylonian Talmud, *Baba Bat'ra* 25b

DAY 346

The Creator of the universe fills all, for the Creator creates
but is Itself not created. The Creator exists in Sky and Earth,
in stone, in everything, even in your heart and in your guts.
As is written: "If a person will hide in the most secret of
places, do you think that I will not see them?" (Jeremiah
23:24). Neither any of the forces of the spirit realm nor of
the earthly realm has ever or can ever see the Creator.
Because what possible power can exist in the created beings
of either the Upper Realms or of the Lower Realms that
would enable their eyes to see what was not created?

—Thirteenth-century RABBI ELIEZER of Worms
in *Sefer So'dey Ra'zeya, Hil'chot HaKavod,* para. 2

DAY 347

How and when were the angels created? By the breath that accompanied God's resonance at the time of creation. As is written: "By the resonance of the Infinite One were the heavens made, and by the breath of God's mouth all of the heavenly forces" (Psalms 36:6). Thus, each time God said "Let there be," or "Earth bring forth living being," angels were created by the breath that carried the sound or resonance of that utterance.

—Thirteenth-century Rabbi Eliezer of Worms
in *Sefer So'dey Ra'zeya, Hil'chot Mal'achim,* para. 1

DAY 348

No creature has ever heard the voice of God. For God does not speak, as one would speak in the mortal sense. Rather, God resonates a single sound, or word, that then splinters into many words, unfolding more and more across time, emerging in timely sequences as a particular communication. Thus, all that God "spoke" over a period of time had already been spoken long ago in a single utterance or resonance that then unfolded gradually over time according to its period of relevance. Therefore, you will not find in our scriptures that God answered someone while in dialogue with them, only that God spoke to them, meaning that yet one more piece of the primal speak emerged in that particular moment, whether in response or otherwise. As is written in the Book of Job: "God resonates many wonders with a single voice" (Job 36:5)—that from one utterance of God emanates myriad wondrous sayings.

—Thirteenth-century RABBI ELIEZER of Worms
in *Sefer So'dey Ra'zeya, Hil'chot HaDibur,* para. 1

DAY 349

The Ten Commandments forbid us from making a graven image of anything that exists in the realm of the heavens or in the realm of the earth (Exodus 20:4). Is this a prohibition against art? Certainly not. Rather, it is a warning against perceiving any creation, whether plant, rock, animal, person, planet, angel, spirit, as its own root source, or as its own source of its own existence and power. Therefore, one must also not take literally the figure of speech employed to describe the various attributes of God, for it is only that: a figure of speech, a meager mortal attempt to grasp in finite terms what is infinite. As is written: "To whom will you compare God? God said: 'To whom will you compare me that I should be equal?'" (Isaiah 40:18 and 25).

—*Sha'ar Hak'domot; Sefer HaRikanti, Vay'chee*

DAY 350

Before you ask God for something, first thank God for what you already have.

—Babylonian Talmud, *B'rachot* 30b

DAY 351

Rabbi Yo'chanan (third century) said in the name of Rabbi Shim'on bar Yo'chai: "Since the time of the Creation of the universe, no one ever thanked God until the matriarch Le'ah did so at the birth of her son Judah: 'This time, I thank God'" (Genesis 29:35). Rabbi El'azar (second century) taught: "From the time of the Creation of the universe, no one ever called God 'Mover of all the Forces,' until Chanah, the mother of the prophet Samuel, addressed God by that attribute."

—Babylonian Talmud, *B'rachot* 30b

DAY 352

We are only here for the weekend. Against the backdrop of billions of years of the existence of our universe, our time on this earth is an unfathomable infinitesimal fraction of fraction of a second. Yet, we each come into this world with the air of an expert, posing great questions of why does this happen, why that, where is God in times of crises, why do the innocent suffer, and so on. It is akin to someone visiting a foreign country for a few hours and griping about the cultural nuances that are alien to his mindset, because he is not learned in the ways of that land or its culture. Likewise is it with being in this life, in this world. Indeed, ask your questions. Complain as you wish. But remember, you just got here, and you are only here for the weekend.

—Rabbi Yisro'el Me'ir Kagan in *Mish'lei Chofetz Chayyim*

DAY 353

There is a time to prolong prayer and a time to shorten prayer. It happened that a disciple led the people in prayer and dragged it out, prolonging the service. A second disciple approached Rabbi El'azar and complained. Rabbi El'azar said: "He isn't prolonging his prayer any more than Moses, as is written, 'And I prayed on the mountain for forty days and forty nights'" (Deuteronomy 9:25). The next day, a different disciple led the people in prayer but shortened it. The same disciple who had complained before, approached Rabbi El'azar once more and complained. Rabbi El'azar said: "He isn't shortening his prayer any more than Moses, as is written, 'And Moses prayed, O God, please heal her'" (Numbers 12:13).

—Babylonian Talmud, *B'rachot* 34a

DAY 354

Any dream, no matter how frightening, can be interpreted for the good. Bar Kapara (third century) asked Rabbi Yehudah Ha'nasi: "I dreamt that my hands were cut off." Rabbi Yehudah said: "It means you will soon no longer have to work so hard with your hands."

—Babylonian Talmud, *B'rachot* 56b

DAY 355

If you see a cat in your dream, a good song is being sung for you. If you see grapes in your dream, it is a good omen. If you see a white horse in your dream, whether running or resting, it is a good omen. If you see a red horse in your dream, if it is resting, it is a good omen, and if it is running, it is a sign of difficulty.

—Babylonian Talmud, *B'rachot* 56b

DAY 356

If you see Yishma'el son of Abraham [the ancestor of the Arabians] in your dream, it is a sign that your prayers are being heard. If you see a camel in your dream, it means you were almost near death and were spared. If you see an elephant in your dream, it implies miracles are about to happen for you, great miracles.

—Babylonian Talmud, *B'rachot* 56b

DAY 357

If you dreamt that you committed adultery, it is a sign that
you are guaranteed an exalted place in the World to Come.
This applies only if there were no adulterous thoughts about
this person during the previous day, or you dreamt of
someone unknown to you.

—Babylonian Talmud, *B'rachot* 57a

DAY 358

If you dreamt about blood, it means prosperity is coming your way and that you will become successful in your livelihood. And if you have no possessions, you will soon inherit some from the least likely source.

—Babylonian Talmud, *B'rachot* 57a

DAY 359

If you dreamt that you were standing naked in Babylon, it is a sign that you lack sin; if you were standing naked in Israel, it means you lack good deeds.

—Babylonian Talmud, *B'rachot* 57a

DAY 360

One does not move a finger Below without the movement of
that finger being enabled from Above. What we choose to do
with our finger or hand, etc., is of course our choice. However
nothing could occur in the first place without the possibility
of having been enabled by the Creator who wills all into
being at every moment.

—Babylonian Talmud, *Chullin* 7b

DAY 361

The Creator is not God, and God is not the Creator. God is more than the Creator and the Creator is but a minute attribute of God who is Infinite. This is likened to the ocean, which is vast, and one cannot see its end, only a small area of it. And if one were to take a stick and create a groove in the sand, only a trickle of the vast ocean would fill it. The ocean is analogous to the infinity of God; the trickle in the groove is analogous to the Creator, which is but a single aspect of the infinity of the great divine mystery we so glibly refer to as God.

—Rabbi Eliezer Benseon Bruk; oral tradition

DAY 362

Come and see, that when God Breath descends to this world, she becomes Soul and passes first through the Mountains of Individuation where she binds with Wind Spirit. Together they continue further toward the earth and bind with Earth Spirit. And in their manifestation they continue to intertwine one with the other until they become as one. Rabbi Yehudah taught: "Wind Spirit and Earth Spirit bind together as one. However, God Breath does not bind with them but dwells deep within the person, waiting to be drawn into union with the other two through a person's deeds and choices."

—*Sefer Ha'Zohar,* Vol. 1, folio 62a

DAY 363

Know that the seventh realm of the heavens is actually one
and the same with the seventh realm of the earth. Both the
heavens and the earth are comprised of seven realms, but the
seventh of each share the very same mystery and are guarded
by the same spirits.

—*Sefer Ha'Zohar,* Vol. 1, folio 40b

DAY 364

Three of the heavenly realms are comprised solely of
women, and no men are permitted there. The first realm is
led by Bat'yah the daughter of Pharaoh, and she leads myriad
thousands of women who merit to bask in her presence.
Three times daily, she conjures the image of Moses and
declares: "Happy is my share in that I raised this Light." A
second Heavenly realm is led by Serach the daughter of
Asher. Three times a day, she conjures the image of Joseph
and runs toward him in celebration, declaring: "How joyful
is that day when through song and dance I delivered the
news to my grandfather Jacob that Joseph was alive!" A third
heavenly realm is led by Yo'cheved the mother of Moses. In
this realm, no images are conjured. Rather, Yo'cheved leads
the women of her realm in song and chant three times
daily, and all who are in the other heavens delight in her
beautiful voice.

—*Sefer Ha'Zohar,* Vol. 4, folio 167b

DAY 365

With the approach of the New Year, we blow our breath through the ram's horn [*sho'far*], to unify the elements of Fire, Wind, and Water, to bring them into a single voice that is the song of Earth. Through this sound we awaken the Voice of the Above so that the song of Heaven joins in unison with the song of Earth until they become one unified resonance that shatters and confuses all the forces of divisiveness. So may it be.

—*Sefer Ha'Zohar,* Vol. 4, folio 99b

INDEX BY DAYS

G

H

ABOUT THE AUTHOR

Gershon Winkler, a longtime practitioner and interpreter of the Kabbalah, teaches workshops on the Kabbalah across the United States, Canada, Europe, and Israel. His most recent book, *Magic of the Ordinary: Recovering the Shamanic in Judaism* (North Atlantic Books), encapsulates his nearly two decades of study and practice of the long-lost shamanic traditions of Judaism. He is cofounder and executive director of the Walking Stick Foundation and Retreat Center in the San Miguel Wilderness of New Mexico where he currently resides. Initiated in Jerusalem in 1978 by the late Kabbalist Rabbi Eliezer Benseon, Winkler has authored thirteen books, primarily on themes related to Jewish theology, folklore, and mysticism. He also conducts monthly seminars on Jewish mysticism and shamanism in Durango, Colorado, and in Albuquerque and Santa Fe, New Mexico, and serves as the itinerant rabbi for Missoula, Montana.